SOCIAL INNOVATION FOR REAL-WORLD TRANSFORMATION

Roadmaps for Changing the World

Julie Chateauvert, Philippe Dufort,
Jonathan Durand Folco, Christopher Gunter,
Krys Maki, Anahi Morales Hudon,
Philippe Néméh-Nombré, Julie Paquette,
Jamel Stambouli, Simon Tremblay-Pepin
and Amanda Wilson

First published in Great Britain in 2025 by

Policy Press, an imprint of
Bristol University Press
University of Bristol
1–9 Old Park Hill
Bristol
BS2 8BB
UK
t: +44 (0)117 374 6645
e: bup-info@bristol.ac.uk

Details of international sales and distribution partners are available at policy.bristoluniversitypress.co.uk

© Julie Chateauvert, Philippe Dufort, Jonathan Durand Folco, Christopher Gunter, Krys Maki, Anahi Morales Hudon, Philippe Néméh-Nombré, Julie Paquette, Jamel Stambouli, Simon Tremblay-Pepin and Amanda Wilson 2025

The digital PDF and ePub versions of this title are available open access and distributed under the terms of the Creative Commons Attribution-NonCommercial-NoDerivatives 4.0 International licence (https://creativecommons.org/licenses/by-nc-nd/4.0/) which permits reproduction and distribution for non-commercial use without further permission provided the original work is attributed.

British Library Cataloguing in Publication Data
A catalogue record for this book is available from the British Library

ISBN 978-1-4473-7473-2 paperback
ISBN 978-1-4473-7474-9 ePub
ISBN 978-1-4473-7475-6 OA PDF

The right of Julie Chateauvert, Philippe Dufort, Jonathan Durand Folco, Christopher Gunter, Krys Maki, Anahi Morales Hudon, Philippe Néméh-Nombré, Julie Paquette, Jamel Stambouli, Simon Tremblay-Pepin and Amanda Wilson to be identified as authors of this work has been asserted by them in accordance with the Copyright, Designs and Patents Act 1988.

All rights reserved: no part of this publication may be reproduced, stored in a retrieval system, or transmitted in any form or by any means, electronic, mechanical, photocopying, recording, or otherwise without the prior permission of Bristol University Press.

Every reasonable effort has been made to obtain permission to reproduce copyrighted material. If, however, anyone knows of an oversight, please contact the publisher.

The statements and opinions contained within this publication are solely those of the authors and not of the University of Bristol or Bristol University Press. The University of Bristol and Bristol University Press disclaim responsibility for any injury to persons or property resulting from any material published in this publication.

Bristol University Press and Policy Press work to counter discrimination on grounds of gender, race, disability, age and sexuality.

Cover design: Liam Roberts Design
Front cover image: istock/ismagilov

Contents

List of figures and tables	iv
Preface	v
Introduction: Learning to change the world	1
1 Innovation beyond buzzwords	13
2 The battlefield of social innovation: strategic challenges and paradoxes	25
3 Understanding the world to change it	40
4 The past as possibilities	50
5 Centering intersectionality and equity	63
6 Acting collectively	74
7 Driving change	83
8 Transforming the economy	92
9 Doing business differently	107
10 Organizing democratically	119
11 Community involvement	126
12 Culture as resistance	134
13 Where do we stand? Unsettling the neoliberal university through engaged pedagogy	146
Conclusion: Changing the scale	158
Notes	167
References	176
Index	194

List of figures and tables

Figures

I.1	Six principles of a just recovery for all	12
3.1	Equality, equity and liberation	43
5.1	The wheel of power and privilege	64
5.2	Feminist intersectionality poster	68
12.1	Public museum model	142
12.2	Ecomuseum model	143

Tables

8.1	Typography of capitalist labor and enterprise	97
9.1	A comparison of classic and social entrepreneurship	111
C.1	The purpose of different strategies	164

Preface

In June 2015, Saint Paul University announced it had received a CAD$2.5 million donation to create a new school of social innovation. Its mandate was to tackle injustices, fight exclusion and reduce poverty in all its forms: economic precarity, marginalization, food insecurity and so on. This school, the first of its kind in Canada, trains youth, professionals, activists and entrepreneurs to foster the development of innovative solutions, local initiatives, community organizations and social enterprises aimed at making the world better.

Beginning in January 2016, a small team of politically engaged professors took on the ambitious challenge of creating a series of academic programs – from bachelors to doctorate – entirely devoted to the emerging field of social innovation. They also established a social innovation workshop, a space of incubation, collaboration and project generation, drawing on models of coworking spaces, innovation labs and other programs to kickstart social enterprises and social organizations.

The CAD$2.5 million donation came from the Sisters of Charity of Ottawa. They hoped that providing these funds would pass on the torch, to continue the mission of changing the world, left by their founder, Élisabeth Bruyère. The Mother Superior of the Sisters of Charity of Ottawa did not content herself with good works and philanthropy. Far from it. As she explained to her team one day, "to fight poverty, we need more than charity and a few attempts to alleviate suffering. We need systems change, and social justice."

This unusual meeting of tradition and modernity, of the church's social values, activist networks and the world of start-ups, may seem unconventional – but innovations often arise at the intersection of different worlds, generating the unprecedented. This trust bestowed by the Sisters of Charity will not lie barren: it remains at the heart of the new school's vision of social innovation. The ultimate aim of the Élisabeth-Bruyère School of Social Innovation is not to create commercially viable businesses "with a human face" that perpetuate the established order but to challenge structures of domination and accelerate social transformation by all means possible.

The new team was quickly confronted with a series of complex questions, both fundamental and inescapable. How can we change the world? What tools, methodologies and strategies are needed to understand social realities, analyze the multiple causes of injustice, explain social change and then launch organizations that are simultaneously viable, effective, democratic and inclusive? How can the social sciences, management studies, activist knowledge and other forms of collective learning be mobilized to promote a blossoming of grassroots initiatives, organizations, social movements, cooperatives and institutions to have a real impact on communities? More fundamentally, what is social innovation?

Because the vision, programs and initiatives of the Élisabeth-Bruyère School of Social Innovation are shaped by active critical reflections on these thorny questions, we decided to take a step back and unpack some of them. How should our school position itself within the theoretical and practical debates around social innovation? How can it contribute, concretely, to the transformation of society? This then is the spirit of our writing project – designed not only to tell our story but to create an accessible guide with concrete suggestions for changing the world.

This translated, revised and expanded version of our *Manuel pour changer le monde* is also an opportunity for us to look inward and reflect. Nearly ten years after the creation of the Élisabeth-Bruyère School of Social Innovation, we believe it's necessary to think about what comes next and share what others might learn from our experiences and experimentations.

The school is, in and of itself, an experiment in social innovation. Not just the school but the research center and nonprofit organization (the Social Innovation Atelier) that make up our bilingual ecosystem; all conceived from within the walls of a university, all with the goal of changing the world. As you might have guessed, at the outset, modesty was not our strength. Our ambition was matched only by our sense of urgency and the necessity to do things differently. And we did. However, our story is not only a story of success. Nearly ten years later, our team has grown to nine full-time professors, along with nearly a dozen part-time professors, two employees at the Atelier and over 100 students; and we've experienced many successes, changes, adaptations.

Our early expansionist views and sense of urgency have been revised with a greater focus on long-term persistence and sustainability. It's possible that we ourselves were victims of a common fallacy of social innovation – assuming that scaling up and growth were signs of success. Much like all instances of social innovation, the implementation of an idea or model must contend with an ever-changing social, political and cultural context and set of circumstances. What has remained constant is our commitment to that overall vision – to create the conditions in which individuals can come together to learn, build capacity and, most importantly, experience social innovation and social transformation. Today, we are more anchored in our shared vision and collectively stronger for the road ahead.

Introduction: Learning to change the world

A world in crisis

In recent years, it has become dangerously banal to point out that the world is in crisis. The environmental crisis, humanitarian crises, loss of trust in institutions, deepening social inequalities, economic precarity and the rise of the extreme right are all symptoms of a world in trouble. Even more disturbingly, part of the problem appears to lie in a hardened belief that there is no alternative, that we are speeding toward collapse, that we cannot fundamentally change the course of things nor act collectively to influence the march of history. The fact that future generations will have a lower quality of life than their parents is increasingly accepted as inevitable, and neofascist governments and political leaders calling for borders to close and rights to be rescinded have become commonplace; the rise of intolerant rhetoric seems to be the only means of stabilizing a visibly disintegrating society. In short, future prospects do not look bright.

In this increasingly precarious context, many people feel it is urgent to act. Things cannot go on this way. We must come up with something – other methods of producing, consuming, housing and relating to others and to the world around us. Myriad community initiatives are springing up: collective gardens, mutual aid systems, local currencies, public markets, solidarity cooperatives, short food supply chains and collaborative platforms. We are also witnessing a resurgence of mobilizations for rights, equality and dignity: Occupy, student movements, #MeToo, Idle No More, Black Lives Matter – not to mention the climate strikes and protests. We are in a time of transition, a calcification of the old order as a new world strives to emerge.

That said, simply observing the existence of alternatives is not enough: they must be nurtured, sustained and multiplied. Movements, energy and ideas are not lacking, but we must strengthen our ability to carry out our projects, make them viable over the long term and increase their scale to achieve a deep transformation of the world. To do so, we must identify, categorize and synthesize priority tools and methods, as well as ways of doing and organizing that have a concrete impact on individuals and communities. While there are no magic bullets, ideal plans or miraculous formulas that can save us once and for all, there are definitely relatively reliable roadmaps – proven strategies that can be mobilized by those seeking change.

At a time when many people no longer believe in the possibility of revolution or political change "from above," a new way forward is on the horizon: we can try to initiate our own plans in the form of social innovations. But what is "social innovation"? Today, it has become quite the buzzword. There's nothing less offensive, positive and remarkable than innovation, especially with a social dimension. Yet, the concept of "social innovation" hasn't always existed, and it doesn't always have the same meaning. Social innovation is used in many ways by many different actors. From the most critical and radical to the most fallacious and sterile, it is particularly confusing when organizations invoke this banner while reproducing the very dysfunctions they claim to resolve. As a first step, we need to clarify different theoretical variations of the contested notion of "social innovation" to better situate ourselves within this fraught terrain.

Between entrepreneurship and emancipation

For starters, we must distance ourselves from the myth of the entrepreneurial hero: the creative, charismatic individual filled with good intentions and ready to go into business and change the world. Currently, a popular discourse, favored by some social entrepreneurs, sees no contradiction between maximizing profit and resolving social problems, perceiving them as two sides of the same coin. In this view of social innovation, businesses play a key role, the market generates new revenue for social causes and private sector efficiency helps boost the nonprofit sector.

From this perspective, it is enough to show a positive attitude, leave conflict and protest behind in favor of win-win solutions and participate in "systemic change" and maximize social impact. Unfortunately, things are not so simple, despite the stories too often heard in business schools.

The Élisabeth-Bruyère School of Social Innovation does not subscribe to this vision of social entrepreneurship, which often presumes social innovation is a new, contemporary idea without history. In fact, there is much we can learn from the past. As we shall see in this book, for centuries, numerous initiatives seeking to address concrete social needs had and continue to have a real influence on history: cooperatives, unions, communes, democratic organizations, self-managed communities, social movements and so on. In short, social innovation didn't start yesterday.

It is also necessary to distinguish the *concept* of social innovation, relatively recent and used in a variety of contexts, from the *social practices* and concrete experiments seeking to change the world through self-organization, mutual aid and collective creativity. While it is important to scrutinize the meaning and trajectories of social innovation within the North American context, where it is marked by an ideology in which the market and entrepreneurship are viewed as magic solutions to all the problems in the world, there are many initiatives emerging in other places and countries that must not be overlooked. In many ways, the West is lagging behind in terms of the development and flourishing of social innovation practices capable of leading to large-scale social transformation.

Before turning more specifically to diverse forms of social innovation and ways we can transform the world, our school sought to develop a general vision, a compass to orient its activities and structure its programs. In our view, an education in social innovation must be both theoretical and practical. It involves learning about, and experimenting with, new organizing models and new social practices, along with an involvement with grassroots struggles against social inequalities and different forms of oppression.

The field of social innovation, as we see it, involves the creation of collective and social enterprises as potential vehicles for change; but it extends far beyond this to include all collective initiatives and experiments seeking to fulfill unmet needs and promote direct democracy and social justice. The fundamental goal of the organizations embodying this social innovation ethos should be to support social movements and other actors of collective change in promoting large-scale social transformation.

Rather than focusing on novelty or measurable impact, the Élisabeth-Bruyère School of Social Innovation emphasizes the importance of taking into account power relations and structures of domination, as well as collective action and the need to unite critical thinking and creativity, social sciences and management techniques and strategies of mobilization and self-management. The values at the heart of its philosophy are critical thinking, leadership, creativity, social engagement and solidarity.

These values and aspirations turn around four main axes, which form the argumentative foundations of this book:

- Develop analytical frameworks enabling a critical understanding of society to identify socially useful projects in a given context. Social innovation gets its meaning and relevance not simply by being new but by responding to a real need, social suffering or problem in society in a way that reshapes structures and relations of power.
- Provide historical knowledge explaining the dynamics of social movements, which lie at the heart of social innovation. The aim here is to understand where organizations involving agents of change are located to help them increase the effectiveness of their actions.
- Develop tools for the democratic management of social organizations in a way that stimulates innovation. Organizational models, collective self-management techniques and the strategic skills needed to start new organizations figure prominently in this axis.
- Link pedagogy and action, research and community involvement. Liberatory pedagogy and action-research aim to unsettle our habits and connect theoretical reflection and practical experience within organizations so that we better

understand the real conditions under which social innovation is produced.

Understanding, explanation, application and action-research thus form the unifying thread of this book, the framework of our social innovation programs and, more broadly, our vision of social transformation.

How to change the world

The outline of this book mirrors our own mapping of roadmaps for social change. Intentionally plural, some of these pathways are necessary prerequisites for further action, while others are complementary strategies that can coexist alongside one another, underscoring the multiplicities of experimentation and variation that are inherent to processes of social transformation.

To better understand the dynamics of social innovation and thereby learn how to transform the structures, institutions and power relations that give rise to unnecessary suffering, we must clear a space for reflection and action. First, we need to understand the origin of the discourse on social innovations, including the historical context in which it emerged and the many, sometimes contradictory, meanings assigned to it depending on the actors involved (Chapter 1).

Outside of what has been said and done in the past around the words "social innovation," how can this concept help people who want to transform society? We suggest that social innovation can be seen through a strategic lens. Inspired by Karl Polanyi and Nancy Fraser, we consider social innovation as a complex relationship between ends and means, one that is always under tension between three polarities: marketization, social protection and emancipation. Still, ours is only one perspective on social innovation. The notion itself has become a contentious battlefield where different approaches compete for legitimacy and power. For some, social innovation is about how to implement private sector practices in organizing charity or social programs. In this regard, social innovation is a way to adapt to neoliberal policies and the rollback of state intervention. Another social innovation, based on emancipatory politics, critiques of systems of domination and self-management of organizations, is possible (Chapter 2).

Next, it is important to highlight certain concepts and analytical tools that can contribute to a better understanding of social realities. Reversing Marx's famous maxim, while it is essential to change the world, we must first understand it well so that transformation moves in the right direction. This involves not only accurately diagnosing current social inequalities and problems but also discovering their causes to be able to go beyond palliative measures and bring about lasting transformation. Moreover, an analysis of social problems cannot be separated from a certain conception of justice and a normative and critical theory able to highlight what is wrong and why changes are necessary (Chapter 3).

If we are to fully understand the structuring of today's world, we will undoubtedly need to look at the past. But while the past informs our critical reading of the world we live in, if we intend to transform our world, it is crucial to distill the past in a useful way. We need to consider the past not only as the accumulation that makes up the present, that is, the texture of the problems we have to deal with today, but also as a repertoire of what was different, what was not yet or not quite, and what could have been possible. Looking at the past, in other words, not only enables us to diagnose but also opens up possibilities for venturing into the otherwise (Chapter 4).

Understanding structures of oppression, how they are created and maintained and how they shape our movements and social organizations is critical to social innovation and change. We look to the foundational work of feminist, critical race theories and intersectional scholars and activists to better understand how individuals hold multiple social identities, which create unique and compelling experiences of both power and oppression. Understanding these intersections and the complexity of how one experiences discrimination, for example, is critical for addressing social inequality in a manner that is both holistic and promotes inclusivity. Understanding one's own positionality and engaging in reflexivity is a practical tool for social movement and innovation work (Chapter 5).

To create change and learn to mobilize, we must understand the mechanisms and strategies of collective action. Social movements have taken multiple forms over the years: labor movements, feminist movements, antiracist movements, decolonial movements, Indigenous movements and so forth. Often reduced to a unidimensional aspect of protest, these movements are in fact linked to a host of social and strategic innovations unfolding through grassroots struggle and ways of coming together, of making claims and of organizing outside institutions to better assert and experiment with other ways of being together, of living, producing, exchanging and inhabiting the world (Chapter 6).

These social movements and the social innovations to which they give rise take shape and spread thanks to their ability to express a message well, to read the social context and to present ideas that resonate with people. This involves an entire labor of framing issues, of forming collective identities and of public communication to make oneself heard and maximize impact on society. This is why it is very useful to understand discursive strategies and the power words have to drive change (Chapter 7).

The economy is a key site of social innovation. Social innovations don't just suggest new solutions within an unchanged economic system; they seek to transform the economy, including our way of understanding it. This involves decentering our gaze so that the market, private enterprise and paid work are not seen as everything. How can the full multiplicity of economic forms, including unremunerated housework, caregiving and community work, be taken into account? How can we rethink the solidarity economy and envisage other ways of eliminating exploitation? How do we look still further and democratize the entire economy (Chapter 8)?

Even after we open up new ways to think about the economy, we still need to learn how to develop, concretely, new forms of economic organization; how to *do business otherwise*. Here we must distinguish between social entrepreneurship and collective entrepreneurship and get acquainted with different forms of social enterprise, from the most conventional to the most original. It is also necessary to learn to start and manage a social enterprise, paying attention to the similarities and divergences between traditional private enterprise and new organizational forms facing the same constraints of competition and funding (Chapter 9).

Once social organizations are launched, the next step is to learn how to work and make decisions together. This requires breaking with the idea that verticality means efficiency and horizontality is impossible. Self-management has a proven track record, and new collaborative management methods give employees greater autonomy to improve management and productivity and to resolve complex problems in creative ways. With a few tricks to facilitate the democratic organization of work and strategic decision making, we open the door to small-scale democracy and nonhierarchical work (Chapter 10).

The workplace is not the only space conducive to such processes. People can also take action in their everyday environments, organizing in these spheres to have a direct impact on their conditions of daily life. This is a matter of reappropriating the power to act on the world, through autonomous community action, renewed forms of participatory and direct democracy, urban or rural land development, taking over empty buildings, converting churches into collective spaces and by many other means. These different regional innovations seek to transform neighborhoods, cities and towns into places where life, supported by local communities, is good for all (Chapter 11).

Social change also needs to tackle the complex issue of "culture," which is a broader reality than arts, music and museums. From a social innovation perspective, culture is a way of life that expresses values and norms through a variety of activities and behaviors that can foster our efforts to socially enhance, empower and change the world around us. Although culture can be a source of oppression as a powerful instrument in the hands of dominant groups, it can also be a source of community empowerment. Local communities and individuals can use culture as a tool to improve everyday life, establishing a record of a people's shared events, their struggles and many victories, and sharing a set of collective values like solidarity, cooperation, honesty, mutual aid and social justice (Chapter 12).

The last chapter is the result of a reflexive analysis of our position in the field, as professors: not primarily as researchers but as teachers. For us, (transgressive) pedagogy – inspired by Paulo Freire, Chandra Talpade Mohanty and bell hooks – is deeply rooted into praxis and is foundational to the ways we engage with the broader community. Against the neoliberalization and corporatization of the university, we believe that pedagogy must be recognized as essential and fundamental to academic work, and we invite you to reflect with us upon our journey to build a place where teaching is anchored by critical reflection on social issues and sits alongside a commitment to change and an openness to the feasibility of making it happen (Chapter 13).

Once the possibility of building a different world on a small scale is apparent, we can ask how a deeper transformation on a larger scale could be envisaged. This is the question of *expanding scale*: moving from local innovation to transforming cultural representations, institutions and even power structures at the societal level. We may naturally think of a managerial approach focused on measuring social impact, but there are other conceptions of social change, relying on a combination of strategies such as ruptural, interstitial and symbiotic transformation, as in American philosopher and sociologist Erik Olin Wright's formulation, a discussion we return to in the Conclusion. Experiments in transition initiatives, resistance, institutional reform and dismantling structures of oppression can contribute to a profound transformation of societal structures. While we don't offer a singular program for macro-level transformation (we don't believe such a program actually exists), we discuss how these on-the-ground initiatives and experimentations might coalesce into something bigger, across both time and space.

We wrote this book from a specific perspective. While each author holds their own set of politics and experiences, we share a commitment to intersectional, decolonial, anticapitalist and antiauthoritarian principles. In our analysis and practice, we strive to center feminist, antiracist, critical disability and 2SLGBTQIA+[1] perspectives. Our perspective is not only shaped by theory but by geography. Where we think and write from is central to explaining the knowledge we produce, and it is essential to clarify and acknowledge it. We currently live in what is known as Canada – or, as it is known by the Indigenous Peoples who have lived here for millennia, Turtle Island – where the Élisabeth-Bruyère School of Social Innovation is located. Specifically, our school is located on the traditional, unceded and unsurrendered territories of the Algonquin Anishinaabe Peoples. Even if, collectively, we bring together a diversity of origins, expertise and identities, the experiences and ideas we reference in this book stem mainly from the Global North. This geographical positioning does not mean that the content of this book only applies to, or is only inspired by, this part of the world. Many examples described in the subsequent chapters are practiced in various contexts, and some of the alternatives put forward in the following pages can also inspire activists and scholars from anywhere.

Living in North America, it is not surprising that many of us are skeptical about the possibility for large-scale, systemic change. As sociologist Gary Kinsman highlights, most of us don't remember the large-scale collective mobilizations of previous decades. This isn't an accident – it is a product of what Kinsman calls the "social organizing of forgetting," whereby dominant social institutions work in such a way as to encourage us to forget the impressive achievements of radical movements that came before us: "We have been forced to forget where we have come from, our histories have rarely been recorded, and we are denied the embodied social and historical literacy that allow us to pass down knowledge, relive our pasts and, therefore, to grasp our present."[2]

We don't remember the incredible organizing of HIV/AIDS activists that led to the creation of the Ontario Trillium Drug Program, which provides public funding for expensive prescription drugs. We forget that farmers across North America organized to resist bank auctions trying to sell off farms during the Great Depression. We forget about the 1919 Winnipeg General Strike, the Days of Action in Ontario in the 1990s, the massive mobilizations against neo-Nazis, the direct action in Clayoquot Sound. The list goes on and on, but we tend to forget, and dominant social institutions and structures encourage us to forget, that collective organizing has a rich past that we can build on and learn from. And that what we're trying to do today is possible, in part, because we did it before.

Further, when we do remember important movements for change, we often perceive them through what political philosopher Angela Davis calls the "heroic individual" discourse, where the gains of movements are attributed to individuals rather than large and diverse movements. We celebrate Gandhi, Martin Luther King, Rosa Parks as impressive individuals rather than leaders and members of rich and powerful collective movements.

In sum, this book attempts to address the exhaustion of utopian energy and the prevailing atmosphere of despair by offering a counterweight and a practical guide to overcoming the multiple challenges facing our world in crisis. People are well aware of looming disasters but feel powerless in the face of the enormity of the task ahead. This book suggests potential solutions. In the spirit of "one no, many yeses," we outline a vast array of possibilities through which to create transformative change within our communities, our cities, our towns and, ultimately, our world. How do we change the world? Through serious and critical reflection, both utopian and pragmatic, anchored in means, tools and strategies tested by concrete action. As Marxist revolutionary Rosa Luxemburg said, "All these conditions cannot be fulfilled by pamphlets and leaflets, but only by the living political school, by the fight and in the fight, in the continuous course of the revolution."[3]

Social transformation in a post-pandemic world

The first edition of this book was written before our worlds were thrown into chaos by the COVID-19 pandemic, when the ways communities came together, social movements organized and the very building blocks of social change were put into question amid widespread lockdowns, evolving public health guidance and an overall climate of fear and uncertainty. At the same time, many social innovations took center stage as communities and grassroots organizations found ways to establish neighborhood mutual aid groups, crowdsource information about vaccine availability and leverage collective power while respecting social distancing requirements. In Canada, a diverse coalition of organizations launched the Just Recovery campaign, urging governments to respond to the pandemic in ways that address long-standing crises and inequities in society (see Figure I.1).

While the pandemic continues to impact many communities, it's fair to say that we've entered a new phase, where some of our activities and routines have returned to the way they were before (for some), while others are still being reimagined and renegotiated. How can we integrate what we've learned into our tools and strategies for social transformation? While this book

Figure I.1: Six principles of a just recovery for all

Source: Corrina Keeling, Just Recovery for All

does not pretend to have the answers, it's clear that the pandemic exposed dangerous and deep-seated fault lines that will need to be addressed if we are to achieve the type of social transformation envisioned in this book.

1

Innovation beyond buzzwords

A short history of a word

Let's start by recalling that the concept of "innovation" has not always had the positive connotation it enjoys today. In 1828, the archaeologist and art critic Antoine-Chrysostome Quatremère de Quincy published *De l'invention et de l'innovation dans les ouvrages des beaux-arts* (On invention and innovation in the fine arts), a book in which he establishes a clear distinction between invention and innovation. While "invention" is defined positively as the "act of reaching a goal one is pursuing and mainly the work of the imagination," the term "innovation" is used "in the unfavorable sense we generally associate with the word innovator."[1] In Quatremère de Quincy's view, the innovator "is focused only on a momentary surprise ... his supposed creation is nothing" because innovation is nothing more than superficial novelty "in the industrial sense, or the sense we attribute to fashion and to everything that is made with a view to performance ... Nothing is new except the date."[2]

Such a distinction can serve as a warning against the superficial uses of this word by marketing and dominant discourse, so fond of change, trends and seductive buzzwords that call on us to embrace novelty – and even planned obsolescence. Social innovation, as we conceive it, must be the work of a real labor of invention and creativity, consisting of developing new means, practices and forms of organization to satisfy social needs while contributing to a real transformation of social relations. However, even this call for social change is not self-evident: it was, in fact, long synonymous with disorder, confusion and chaos. As historian Benoît Godin remarks: "For centuries ... the word innovation was a damned word, a pejorative."[3]

How did we evolve from a world in which innovation was viewed with suspicion, an eccentricity, even a danger to the establishment, to a society that embraces it at every turn, innovation having been elevated to the supreme value of technological, economic and social development? According to Godin, this transition from pejorative label to positive value took place during the shift from traditional to modern societies:

> Innovation was prohibited by church decree ... speeches and sermons, religious and political, denounced innovation. In England, the *Book of Prayer* enjoined people to not take part in the "folly" of man and get mixed up in "the latest innovations." At the time, bishops would visit the parishes to ensure these prohibitions were respected. The meaning of the concept changed in the modern era. The meaning shifted as innovation came to be considered as contributing to meeting men's needs and to achieving their goals – moral, political, social and material. Henceforth, innovation became a concept that served narratives, in the broad sense of the term, and allowed both past and present to be interpreted, in a positive way.[4]

Not until the end of the 20th century did innovation emerge as central to our model of development. During the 1980s and 1990s, the liberalization of markets, the global circulation of capital and goods and then the information and communication technologies revolution accelerated the process of globalization. In a context marked by strong interstate competition, in which scientific policy, research and development and the knowledge economy played an increasing role, the imperatives of productivity, growth and technological development placed innovation at the heart of the economic system.

During this period, "the notion of innovation developed within the world of technology and was part of a market logic in which the enterprise was the prime breeding ground. The tight proximity between 'innovation' and 'technology' was such that it was rarely specified by name that it was technological innovation."[5] This symbiotic relationship between innovation and technology gave way to a proliferation of meanings in a host of fields. We began to speak of innovation in organizations, media, culture, art and regions, to the point of no longer knowing what exactly we were discussing.

Alongside technical, industrial and economic innovations aimed at marketing new products, services and gadgets, the social sciences, social economy and grassroots initiatives started to proclaim that they too are being innovative, for social ends. Innovations are no longer solely a means of increasing the productivity of the labor process or the competitiveness of a company but are new ways of promoting justice, reducing poverty, protecting the environment and rebuilding social ties in a world marked by isolation, precarity and inequalities.

Social innovations thus often arise in a context of crisis, where the established socioeconomic order is no longer able to meet the expectations of individuals in terms of work, inclusion and standard of living. Existing solutions fail, institutions no longer reflect reality in their functioning, cracks appear in the system and new aspirations emerge. As political scientist Janine Brodie reflects, drawing on Karl Polanyi, a time of crisis "unleashes myriad alternative political and social imaginaries, some built on the injuries of social inequalities, others focused on shoring up the crumbling edifices of common sense, and still others promoting transformative visions of more equitable and sustainable futures."[6]

A response to neoliberalism

In the 1980s, Western societies entered the era of neoliberalism. An economic and political project centering on the freedom of enterprise, the privatization of public goods, free trade, individual responsibility and entrepreneurship, neoliberalism helped to challenge the gains made under the welfare state and the public management of the economy to the benefit of private interests. Privileging a conception of the human being as *Homo economicus* – a calculating individual evolving in a world of competition – neoliberalism represents a *vision of the world* in which there is neither society nor any viable alternative.[7]

The progressive introduction of this model of development fostered the deregulation of the financial sector, the concentration of wealth, the domination of giant multinationals and an explosion of economic inequalities.[8] Since the first privatizations and social reversals were imposed by Augusto Pinochet in Chile in the 1970s, and Margaret Thatcher in the UK and Ronald Reagan in the US in the 1980s, a multitude of austerity measures, public service cuts, public–private partnerships and market-based mechanisms in public institutions have contributed to the near hegemonic spread of neoliberal logic.

These changes were particularly harmful to poor communities who relied on the social safety net (welfare, social services and so on) and were now pushed further into poverty and criminalized.

> As the state withdraws from a range of areas with respect to social reproduction, it promotes private individual and family responsibility, rather than a sense of collective responsibility for these activities. These costs, however, are disproportionately borne by women and the poor, and the lack of social provision creates new forms of inequality.[9]

While the specific manifestation of neoliberalism differs across regions and contexts, taken together we can understand the imposition of neoliberalism as an attempt to fundamentally alter our relationship to each other and the world as a whole. As philosopher Pierre Dardot and sociologist Christian Laval emphasize:

> What is at stake is nothing less than *the form of our existence*; that is, the way that we are pressured to behave and to relate to others and ourselves. Neoliberalism in fact defines a certain standard of life in Western societies and, far beyond, in all societies who follow them on the path of "modernity." This norm calls on everyone to live in a world of generalized competition; it summons populations to enter into

economic struggle with each other, it orders social relations according to the model of the market, its transformation extends to the individual, now called to conceive of themselves as enterprises.[10]

This is the historical context in which social innovations, as we conceive of them today, emerged. The state's withdrawal from funding social programs in favor of increased surveillance and punishment and the ongoing blind spots of the market created spaces in which a blossoming of local initiatives, community innovations and collective experiments emerged to meet the many essential needs for care, food, labor market integration and other local services. In the face of triumphant individualism, globalization and the imperative to compete, another logic emerged, one based on collective self-organization, mutual aid and reciprocity, crafting practical solutions to meet the urgent needs of communities both discarded and targeted by neoliberal ideologies.

For this reason, researchers Jacques Nussbaumer and Frank Moulaert believe that social innovation:

> offers a constructive response to the economist and technologist vision of economic development dreamed about and implemented by neoliberals. It defends a [vision] of solidarity, cooperation and (human, cultural and economic) diversity and of solutions to the problems of human development ... The concept of social innovation seeks to reconstruct social links outside of, or in combination with, the market.[11]

That said, the relationship between social innovation and neoliberalism is complex. While social innovation often seems to be a solidarity-based response to problems caused by "the whole market," it is also an extension of corporate logic into the nonprofit sector and social practices aimed at social change. The popularity of the term "social innovation" corresponds precisely to the last big global financial crisis of 2007–08. The failure of the neoliberal project thus brings about the need to renew capitalism, to make it more "sustainable," "responsible," "moral" and "inclusive."

Since then, the rise of social entrepreneurship, the collaborative economy and new organizational forms, such as social businesses, helped to blur the lines between private enterprise, social economy and traditional community sector projects.[12] Social innovation, now promoted by business schools, private foundations, governments, start-up incubators and impact investment funds, seems to be linked to other phenomena, such as corporate social responsibility and digital platforms, like Uber and Airbnb, in a catchall that makes it difficult to orient oneself. If any new product, service or organization with a supposedly positive impact on society is defined as social innovation, how can we distinguish the wheat from the chaff?

Like other trendy words such as "participation," "empowerment," "transition," "governance," "diversity" and "sustainable development," social innovation is assigned different meanings by the various actors, institutions and discourses mobilizing the term. Far from being a simple "floating signifier," this elastic notion currently seems to be associated with three main types of discourses or visions: neoliberal, social democratic and radical critique. We will sketch a quick portrait of each conception to situate the Élisabeth-Bruyère School of Social Innovation within this constellation.

The emergence of social neoliberalism

In the first place, the neoliberal conception of social innovation is part of a broad process of *commodification*, that is, the general extension of market logic to institutions, social practices and interpersonal relationships. While social innovations are often perceived as collective responses to the destructive impact of neoliberalism, neoliberal rationality has *also* had the effect of shaping social innovation according to corporate logic, positioning *social enterprises* and *social entrepreneurship* as magic solutions to the great ills of society. Thus, this vision advocates for the creation of new businesses with a human face as the response to pressing social issues, endowing the traditional model of the private enterprise with a new social purpose.

Unlike classic neoliberalism, which is based exclusively on competition and individual interest, a new form of *social neoliberalism* has grown out of the transformation of the welfare state, encouraging members of society to combine their economic interests and community involvement and take charge of the social safety net themselves.[13] This downloading onto communities reproduces precarious low wage work, particularly for women and women of color, who make far less than their counterparts who previously performed this work in the public sector. In a context of austerity, this transfer of responsibility onto individuals is part of a commodification of social demands whereby individuals are now called upon to create social enterprises to mitigate the deficiencies of the market and state redistribution. This dynamic unfolds as a dual process of the humanization of the corporation and the *corporatization* of the social.[14]

Indeed, geographers Jamie Peck and Adam Tickell highlight that part of the evolving neoliberal discourse has been the use, and perversion of, notions of community, self-help and community empowerment:

> [The] selective appropriation of "community" and nonmarket metrics, the establishment of social-capital discourses and techniques, the incorporation (and underwriting) of local-governance and partnership-based modes of policy development and program delivery in areas like urban regeneration and social welfare, the mobilization of the "little platoons" in the shape of (local) voluntary and faith-based association in the service of neoliberal goals, and the evaluation of invasive, neopaternalist modes of intervention (along with justifications for increased public expenditure) in areas like penal and workfare policy.[15]

Some scholars, such as Nathan Farrell, go so far as to talk about the emergence of *conscious capitalism* and the neoliberalization of the nonprofit sector to describe this phenomenon of the repositioning of capitalism and the corporation in the market of moral conscience, inclusion and social impact.[16] This dynamic facilitates the introduction of management theories and the lexicon of private enterprise into community organizations, collective enterprises and other civil society organizations. The idea is to place capitalism at the service of humanity, to adopt the famous formulation of Muhammad Yunus, regarded as the inventor of microcredit and an icon in social entrepreneurship circles.[17]

In the same vein, funding from private foundations and government grants have introduced mechanisms to measure quantified "social impact" and performance indicators to determine the social and economic profitability of investments. While it is not possible to describe this form of neoliberal social innovation in any depth here, we can briefly note that it is currently the dominant approach in the West. It is promoted by several influential organizations, such as the McConnell Foundation, the *Stanford Social Innovation Review*, Ashoka, Yunus Social Business and the Young Foundation. As the evocative title of a book by Matthew Bishop, journalist and social entrepreneur, and Michael Green, Executive Director of the Social Progress Imperative, emphasizes, we live in an era of "philanthrocapitalism," which integrates tools of finance capitalism into the world of philanthropy and social entrepreneurship.[18]

Social economy and social democracy

In contrast to the neoliberal approach, which is based on philanthropic solidarity, benevolence, individual solutions and market mechanisms, another concept of social innovation has roots in 19th-century workers' and cooperative movements. Jean-Louis Laville, professor in solidarity economies, describes the emergence of the social and solidarity economy through the creation of cooperatives, mutuals, mutual aid groups and other collective organizations as a response to the dysfunctionality of nascent industrial capitalism.[19]

In the 20th century, this type of economy, based on cooperation, self-organization, social justice and democratic solidarity, evolved through autonomous community and grassroots initiatives in Quebec, Canada; the popular economy and informal sector in Latin America; as well as new organizational forms, such as social cooperatives in Italy and collective interest cooperatives in France.[20] Unlike Western *social enterprises*, which may still be for-profit private enterprises, the social economy includes *collective enterprises* (cooperatives, associations, mutuals and so on) that have a social purpose, aim to meet the needs of their members or the community, embrace democratic governance and aspire to economic viability.[21]

While the neoliberal approach represents a microsocial (even individualistic) conceptualization of social innovation, emphasizing the role of entrepreneurship and the enterprise as the engine of change and innovation, the social-democratic vision views the social economy as a way to fill the gaps within public services, to ensure social cohesion and renew the role of the welfare state. The latter "would be present less as an overall planner and more as a partner of the private sector and the social economy … In this context, the state is called upon to play a catalyzing role promoting the multiplication of agreements between economic and non-economic partners."[22]

In this spirit of collaboration among private, public and community sectors, the social-democratic model recognizes the social economy through laws, public policies and sustainable forms of funding. For example, in Quebec, there is an entire ecosystem involving various organizations and networks that fund and support this model of social innovation. There are also the examples of the first self-managed daycares, community clinics and other initiatives that came out of the 1970s grassroots movements and were gradually institutionalized in the 1980s and 1990s. This social-democratic conception is thus part of a larger approach of *institutional recognition* and *social protection*, in which governments play a central role.

This conceptualization of social innovation does not necessarily aim to transform the established order; rather, it tries to compensate for the shortcomings of the state and market by offering other services to address housing, poverty and various forms of social exclusion. For instance, in Quebec, the institutionalization of the social economy was a compromise among unions, bosses and the state during the 1996 Summit on the Economic and Social Future of Quebec, at a time when then premier Lucien Bouchard subscribed to a zero deficit policy. The social economy thus could not claim to replace private enterprises or public services; it primarily aimed to be recognized as an entirely separate sector of the economy, useful for job creation and social solidarity. We thus adhere to the analysis of political scientist Gabriel Arsenault on this point: "We will characterize the dominant conception of the social economy in Quebec as centre-*left*: centre, because the social economy is generally conceived here as complementary rather than alternative to the private and public sectors; centre-left, because it primarily serves values associated with the left, such as equality and solidarity."[23]

In contrast to the centrist or even right-wing ideological orientation of entrepreneurial social innovation, social innovations that are part of a social-economy and social-democratic perspective often adopt a logic of consultation, partnership, good governance, territorial development and citizen participation with the goal of ending economic precarity and overcoming the failings of neoliberalism.[24] That said, they rarely challenge the establishment or structures of domination such as capitalism, colonialism, sexism, racism and so on. At the end of the day, social-democratic social innovations are more about correcting existing inequalities through the recognition of the social economy as a distinct economic sector.

Liberatory model

A third, more "radical" conceptualization of social innovation is grounded in the logic of collective action, aiming at deeper social transformation. The underlying principle is no longer the market or the private enterprise, nor recognition or consultation by the state, but collective self-organization by social actors and marginalized groups seeking to combat social injustices and dynamics of exclusion. From this perspective, the goal is not *only* to resolve social problems with new solutions but to transform the conditions of existence of communities and dismantle structures of domination. In other words, the goal is not solely to respond to specific needs but to orient social practices toward a larger emancipatory project. As Marie-Hélène Bacqué, scholar in urban studies, and economist Carole Biewener note:

> The goal of individual and collective emancipation leads into a project of social transformation which, in the most radical approaches, is based on a challenge

of the capitalist system. Schematically, this conception of empowerment assumes its meaning in a chain of equivalencies linking notions of justice, redistribution, social change, consciousness-raising and power, the latter exercised by those below.[25]

In contrast to the dominant logic of the contemporary social economy sector, the liberatory model takes up the tradition of the workers' movement, the *solidarity* economy and democratic socialism, which aim at a broader democratization of the economy.[26] In general, social innovations are not primarily seen in this view as the product of the entrepreneur or a third sector, meeting needs that are left unsatisfied by the market and the state, but as the expression of social movements prefiguring new forms of organization, production and consumption.

This form of social innovation, still in the minority, in some ways continues the experiences of the collective self-organized (or *autogestion*) movements of the 1960s and 1970s in their attention to power relations, the concern for radical democracy and the goal of a new, postcapitalist social order. The resurgence of the idea of the "commons"[27] and the principle of collective autonomy, visible in projects such as Bâtiment 7 in the Pointe St Charles neighborhood of Montreal, Quebec,[28] provide an insight into this form of social innovation that often emerges in the aftermath of significant popular struggles. The transition town movement, intentional communities and other projects to localize the economy contribute to this mix of protest, autonomy and alternative culture aiming to change the world without taking power.[29]

As you will see in this book, the professors at the Élisabeth-Bruyère School of Social Innovation mainly subscribe to this liberatory perspective of social innovation. That said, even the most liberatory social innovation projects often take the form of collective enterprises that are part of the larger field of social economy. Sometimes even social entrepreneurs who, out of necessity, adopt a lexicon of neoliberalism and social impact with funders manage to carry out astonishingly radical projects with a notable transformative impact.

This is why it is important to keep in mind the complexity of social innovation projects, which evolve in a world filled with contradictions. Overly hasty categorizations of actors into "evil capitalism," "soft center" or "radical left" should be avoided. Neoliberal, social-democratic and liberatory conceptions are *theoretical models* that serve to differentiate dynamics in a controversial and complex field, and they generate a host of hybridizations and intersections of all kinds. The objective here is not to put each approach to social innovation on trial but to directly answer the following question: How, seriously, can we change the world?

2

The battlefield of social innovation: strategic challenges and paradoxes

We ended our last chapter on a distinction between three types of social innovation: neoliberal, social democratic and liberatory. This division is based on the goals of social innovation and how they are managed and conceptualized. As we saw, this can be a very useful distinction, but it might be an over-simplification compared to the messiness of real-world problems. This framework produces the following questions: What do people who are involved in these projects want? What are the goals, tools, discourses, governance models and resources they mobilize to realize their ideas?

We all know from experience that our goals do not always turn out exactly as planned when we try to realize them in the real world. We also know that some people sometimes pretend to have the most laudable of intentions, but when they implement them, their projects have the opposite effects. So, could we judge the tree of social innovation by the fruits it bears? What effects do social innovation projects have on the community or the society where they take place? An argument can be made that only social innovation initiatives that succeed in building a better world for everyone qualify as "liberatory."

This chapter presents a more concrete, practical and strategic approach to social innovation, inspired by ideas from Karl Polanyi, Nancy Fraser and Pierre Bourdieu, to understand the relationship between social innovation and its complex effects on society. This approach helps us to explain the problems practitioners of social innovation face when they are trying to change the world from the field of social innovation and what strategies they might deploy to overcome those problems.[1]

Polanyi and the double movement

Social innovation as a field is interested in organizational initiatives from individuals and communities attempting to solve their political, cultural, ecological or socioeconomic problems by mobilizing the resources at their disposal. Most social innovation studies focus primarily on short-term local dynamics while ignoring the systemic social forces that drive the world we live in.

To evaluate the social impact of local initiatives, we need a bigger picture to understand more global social transformations. In the face of today's structural, ecological, socioeconomic and democratic crises, transition calls for a theorization of the roots of systemic change. Polanyi's work proposes studying the relationship between economic and social structures to understand how the market transforms society. His work *The Great Transformation* is enjoying a resurgence in popularity today, mainly because we face challenges similar to those Polanyi observed in the 1940s related to the crisis of market society, the rise of populist and far-right movements, wars and the need to take back control over large economic processes.[2]

Polanyi traces a history that emphasizes social struggles and proposes a rearranging of the historical narrative around a double movement opposing, on the one hand, social forces favoring the commodification of society and, on the other, social movements aimed at social protection against the disintegrating effects of the market. The "double movement thesis" is rooted in the historical development of the capitalist system, which Polanyi sees through the expansion and deepening of market social relations or "commodification." His narrative focuses on the "self-regulating market" and its attempt to subordinate social institutions, morality and ethics to a narrow economic logic.

The first movement of commodification implies that the market gradually becomes autonomous from the constraints of society. The economy – which was embedded within society (its rules, values, institutions and so on) in noncapitalist societies – would gradually be extracted from society through the establishment of liberal institutions and an autonomous, "self-regulated" logic. Polanyi refers to these social transformations in his concept of the "disembedding of the economy," enabling the transition to capitalism and "free market society."

The profound macrosocial upheavals engendered by this disembedding causes multiple problems within society: growing economic inequalities, the erosion of social cohesion, the destruction of ecosystems and public goods and so on. Those crises set in motion a "countermovement" of communities, social groups and institutions that react directly to the corroding dynamic of the market to "protect society" and create a new equilibrium where communities might find a stable way to thrive. Proponents of the unregulated market in the 19th century and the present day set up movements to bring down social protection laws. The Polanyian narrative, on the other hand, presents social groups and movements as trying to resist the effects of commodification. The joint social effect of these forces is to "re-embed" the market within nonmarket institutions, ethics and morals. They support the second Polanyian movement called the "social protection" movement. This double movement is at the heart of *The Great Transformation*'s theoretical proposition.

However, this Polanyian approach remains limited in the sense that it gives the dynamics of commodification too central a role, while other systems of power and the major social processes that correspond to their evolution are secondary. It's here that Fraser's rereading of this double movement overcomes this reductionism by restoring agency to all social movements aiming at emancipation in the face of forms of injustices that do not rest in the idea of the market.[3]

Fraser and the emancipation movement

Feminist philosopher Nancy Fraser claims that the social relations related to "social protection" are not exempt from domination. Traditional forms such as the family, the village, the clan or the nation offer possible spaces for protecting the social bond in the face of the atomization caused by commodification. However, these same social bonds are often infused with forms of oppression that preceded capitalism, such as sexism, racism and colonialism. These systems of oppression have their own history and dynamics. Capitalism then becomes entangled with them, often deepening their logic of domination (heteropatriarchal, racist, colonial). In formulating the framework of his narrative, Polanyi relegates all these dynamics to the background of his work. Implicit in his plot is a prescriptive message that society must be defended against commodification. Fraser's feminist rereading attempts to overcome this reductionism by proposing to put these social movements upfront when considering the structuring effects of systems of power other than capitalism.[4]

To this end, Fraser proposes including a third pole to Polanyi's theoretical framework, emancipation, which refers to all the social struggles that resist systems of domination, such as the women's movement, 2SLGBTQIA+ struggles, Indigenous decolonization movements, Black liberation movements and animal rights movements. The historical narrative is thus structured around a triple movement including social forces supporting commodification, social protection and emancipation.

Emancipation aims to remove oppression from both market and nonmarket interactions. According to Fraser, the social movements that drive emancipation are those that fight oppressive social norms across the board, regardless of whether these norms respond to market dynamics.[5] This leads emancipatory social movements both to align themselves with the social protection movement, in cases where it opposes economic exploitation or serves emancipatory solidarities, and to oppose it in cases where it protects oppressive social norms such as patriarchy or racism. Emancipatory struggles sometimes converge with the aims of advocates of commodification, particularly when their goal is to abolish social protections with an oppressive dimension. They can also converge with the social protection movement when they seek to oppose the oppressive effects of market deregulation. This perspective is particularly suited to contextualizing attempts by social innovation organizations to disrupt power structures. These theoretical foundations place these paradoxical relationships at its heart and allow us to develop the concept central to our theoretical proposition: social effect.

The notion of social effect

While the notion of *social impact* is often used in the universe of social innovation, aiming to maximize one's end results at specific actors or beneficiaries, the theoretical approach built on Polanyi's and Fraser's insights allows us to see the broader influence of social factors like commodification, social protection and emancipation. This is why Philippe Dufort, one of the founders of the Élisabeth-Bruyère School of Social Innovation, argued that we need to replace the fuzzy language of *social impact* with a more precise language of *social effects*.[6] A social effect of commodification atomizes society and establishes the market as the mediator of social bonds and the main relationship to nature. A social protection effect preserves nature and the social fabric in the face of commodification and constructs modalities that enable solidarity without taking into account the possible dynamics of oppression underlying this solidarity. On the other hand, a social effect of emancipation subjects all social ties to critique and aims to dissolve its oppressive structures, regardless of the solidarity ties affected. The concept of social effect thus becomes the basis for understanding the complexity of organizational practices that bring about social innovations. It's important to clearly distinguish the idea of social effect from the sociopolitical purpose of organizations and social movements. A sociopolitical purpose is conjunctural and represents a specific, limited objective, while the notion of social effect grasps the structural transformations resulting from social innovation projects.

The organizational paradoxes of social innovation

We can now turn to conceptualizing a preoccupation that marks the daily lives of most social innovation practitioners: navigating the organizational paradoxes resulting from an inscription in, against and beyond various power structures, including the market.[7] Indeed, even if organizations have a primary affiliation with only one of these poles of the triple movement, practitioners' daily work is simultaneously embedded in the entanglements of commodification, social protection and emancipation movements. The process of mobilizing resources in this complex setting often entails major complications for organizations. Indeed, the simultaneous interweaving of antagonistic social effects leads to tensions within organizations that aim to change the world. By simultaneously supporting two incompatible logics in an effort to acquire resources, the social effects produced by the organization might become paradoxical. For practitioners, this reality causes ethical, political and interpersonal headaches.

This brings us back to our discussion of the challenges faced by practitioners in acquiring resources on a day-to-day basis to transform dominant structures. Many social innovations that have led to large-scale social effects are the result of hybridization practices. Take, for example, athlete Colin Kaepernick's advertising campaign for Nike, which capitalized on the commodification of social commitment to spread an antiracist message.[8] These hybridizations, which may seem ludicrous from a political or ethical point of view, take their coherence from a strategic calculation aimed at transforming the "initial balance of power" in a context favoring conservative organizations.

It is important to conceptualize the various organizational strategies seeking systemic change. Organizations capable of transforming the "macrosocial level" must excel in the "art of creating power." They must deploy strategies at the organizational level that enable them to acquire ever more structural power, influence and resources. In concrete terms, this means accumulating enough money and putting together enough people for the organization to have the power to change the world around it according to the organization's goal. Practitioners of social transformation know all too well the constant compromises and tensions involved in their strategies for changing the world. Indeed, as the strategies of oppressed groups are often based on the hybridization of resources that result in paradoxical social effects, the art of creating structural power causes many challenges for the managers of these organizations.

Strategic drift

This framework, inspired by Polanyi, Fraser and Dufort, allows us to better understand the *strategic drift* of organizations. Often called *mission drift*, strategic drift happens when an organization engages in dynamics specific to a secondary social effect to obtain certain resources, but this secondary social effect gradually becomes the organization's primary social effect. For example, a social enterprise that first aims to help graduate students overcome loneliness and anxiety by offering writing retreats and workshops to increase productivity and well-being might end up having a more commercial focus (the commodification movement) by maximizing its profits over students' well-being.

Drift is a constant risk in the field of social innovation. Let's take another concrete example. An organization born of an emancipatory social innovation, channeling market resources toward the fight against gender discrimination, may fall victim to its commercial success and, for a variety of internal dynamics, come to prioritize the market objective. On the other hand, this same organization, if it had chosen to rely on preexisting forms of solidarity such as nationalism, may eventually develop oppressive practices if protectionist identity cleavages come to frame certain immigrant women as a threat to national identity. These are examples of how an initial strategic choice can, over time, lead to the drifting process (some would prefer the term *cooptation*).

This theoretical approach enables us to understand the complex interactions between social effects within organizations that aim to change the world. The main practical advantage of this conceptualization is to grasp the opportunities offered by hybridizations to acquire structural power and achieve systemic change while shining a light on the ethical problems they can create in practice and the risks of strategic drift. If the goal of emancipatory social innovation is to change the world, this task will not be fulfilled without its practitioners facing puzzling problems and dangerous threats. Understanding how they manage to overcome them (or not) should be central to the study of liberatory social innovation.

In the previous sections, we analyzed social innovation as processes emerging from practitioners facing organizational problems and paradoxes and strategizing to address them. Nevertheless, the approach based on "social effects" does not grasp social innovation as an institutionalized field or arena of social interaction. The approach of the "triple movement" analyzes social innovation processes in terms of their effects, that is, as something that has certain complex impacts, without asking what the words "social innovation" mean for the actors that lead projects, the organizations that fund those projects, the professionals who support them and so on. Social innovation is not just a thing or a process but can also be understood as a set of social relations taking shape in a space traversed by power relationships, or in other words, as a "field."

What is a field?

The interpretation of social innovation as a field was first formulated by sociologist Yves-Marie Abraham.[9] In this view, the field designates:

> a subset of social space that is constituted by a struggle for the accumulation of a specific form of capital. The agents (individuals, organizations) involved in this competitive space are unequally endowed with capital – there are dominants and dominated. Although they are in competition with each other, the agents in question have a vested interest in the perpetuation of the field. These agents also have sociological characteristics – habitus – that are more or less adapted to the rules of the game in force in the field. Their strategies depend on their position in the field and their habitus.[10]

This vision brings into play the notions of capital and habitus, which are central categories in the work of French sociologist Bourdieu. By capital, we mean a certain stock of resources that enables the individual to act and exercise power in a defined sphere of social life. Economic capital (material wealth, profits, assets) is well known, but there is also cultural capital (knowledge, diplomas, general culture), social capital (networks of relationships and the ability to mobilize them) and symbolic capital (recognition, prestige, social esteem). It is worth noting that social innovators, social entrepreneurs and activists all need those different forms of capital to realize their projects.

For example, economic capital is needed to build an organization like a nonprofit or cooperative, and the actors might gather resources from grants, loans, gifts, crowdfunding platforms or memberships. On the other hand, implementing a social innovation project often requires a diversity of expertise, know-how and talents, making it necessary to build teams made up of individuals with a certain level of cultural capital. Acquiring economic resources and good collaborators requires networking and social capital, both of which represent a way to get access to opportunities or to mobilize local communities to support new projects. Finally, it is essential to establish the credibility of the team or project leader through various forms of symbolic capital to establish the legitimacy of the project and thus increase its chances of being financed.

Capital is acquired through the presence of habitus – acquired dispositions or habits (skills, styles, tastes, tacit knowledge) that enable players to interact effectively and position themselves well in their field. It should be noted here that the different forms of capital are not necessarily interchangeable: economic capital does not naturally transform into intellectual capital. For example, being rich doesn't automatically make you knowledgeable or intelligent.

Another characteristic of fields is that it is the dominant or established players who try to preserve the rules of the game to maintain their privileges, while players in a minority position or outsiders try to dislodge them by challenging the rules of the game. The same is true in the religious, political and literary fields, where different currents clash over the very definition of the field.

And yet, despite the fierce power struggles, rivalries and antagonisms that characterize each field with its specific dynamics, there is always a common issue or force that brings all players together within the field. In the specific context of social innovation, all players and organizations recognize that there are major social issues and problems and needs that are not yet being met, for example. Hence, all people working in the social innovation field believe that we need to come up with new ideas, solutions, practices and ways of doing things to bring about improvements, positive changes and "to modify social relations, transform a framework for action or propose new cultural orientations," as the definition from CRISES (the Center for Research on Social Innovations at the University of

Quebec-Montreal) recalls.[11] All the players involved in social innovation, from activist groups to major private banks, civil servants and university research centers, agree on these broad ideas. The main goal of the field is to bring about social impact, social change or systemic change.

Strategic action fields

American sociologists Neil Fligstein and Doug McAdam developed the theory of strategic action fields, which can help us understand concrete dynamics in the arena of social innovation. These authors conceive of fields as spaces animated by social actors evolving in a troubled world and seeking legitimacy while emphasizing the power relations within the field that lead to various forms of struggle, conflict and contestation over established rules.[12] A strategic field of action is defined as an intermediate-level social order in which actors (individuals or collectives) expect to interact with each other on the basis of (a) shared understandings about the purposes of this field, (b) relationships with other actors in the field (including those with more power) and (c) rules that define legitimate actions in this field.[13]

Unlike Bourdieu's approach, which emphasizes the search for capital and the accumulation of power, Fligstein and McAdam's perspective emphasizes the key role of collective representations or shared understandings called *interpretive frameworks* (or discourses, worldviews).

The degree of consensus or contestation within a given field varies over time, and the balance of forces shifts according to circumstances and relationships with other fields. Whereas Bourdieu's theory focuses on a single field in isolation, Fligstein and McAdam's theory recognizes the plurality, interlocking and interdependence of diverse social fields, such as the economic field, the political field, the academic field. Fields are not static, eternal spaces but social arenas whose boundaries, rules and dynamics evolve according to the field's internal interactions, overlaps with other fields and broader societal dynamics. In contrast to Bourdieu's approach, which focuses on competition between different players in the same field, Fligstein and McAdam's approach emphasizes the role of cooperation and the coalitions that take shape within it. The more a field is marked by an unequal distribution of economic and symbolic resources, the more this field will tend to be organized hierarchically, fostering power struggles within it.[14]

Fields: resonance and interdependence

Strategic action field theory also emphasizes the important role of "internal governance units" in maintaining order within a particular field. Governance units play a variety of roles: stabilizing the field; responding to crises affecting the field; acting as intermediaries with other fields such as business, government, the community sector and so on. At the microsocial level, Fligstein and McAdam emphasize the "existential function of the social," that is, the deeply human need to create meaningful social worlds and develop feelings of belonging.[15] For them, social actors are not primarily or solely driven by self-interest or the quest for power or recognition but by the need to "make sense" of the world. This existential function of the social plays a very strong role among the new generations, and particularly in the field of social innovation: "I want my work to have meaning," "I want to make a difference," "I want my actions to have a positive impact on the world" and so on. To build coalitions, forge identities and bring interests together to carry out projects, changemakers need social skills that enable them to call upon shared meanings, empathically relate to others, induce collaborative practices and foster collective action.[16] To borrow the terminology of philosopher and sociologist Hartmut Rosa, social actors seek above all "resonance" with others and the world around them.[17]

Finally, Fligstein and McAdam's great contribution to field theory is their conceptualization of the relationships between fields. Instead of focusing exclusively on the internal dynamics of the social innovation field, for example, it is useful to conceive of this emerging field as nested within a complex set of other fields with which it maintains greater or lesser links of dependence: the field of philanthropy, the field of finance, the field of municipal and national government and so on. The various fields may be nested like "Russian dolls," forming networks of interdependence or connection with other fields to a greater or lesser degree.[18]

The social innovation field

How can we understand the field of social innovation, with its history and internal tensions? A strategy might be to look at its interdependencies with other proximate fields, such as philanthropy, the social economy, social entrepreneurship, social finance, the community milieu and territorial development.[19] While being connected to those various spheres, the social innovation field is in the process of institutionalization, with its own rules, frameworks of interpretation, norms, practices, modes of financing, units of governance and established interests. As the theory of strategic fields of action points out, it is precisely the importance of relations between fields and the phenomena of boundaries and crossovers that contribute to the emergence of new fields with shifting boundaries.[20]

In a nutshell, what makes up the field of social innovation? At the microsocial level, there are first and foremost "changemakers" who mobilize resources (economic, social and symbolic) to carry out projects aimed at meeting social challenges or needs from a perspective where improving collective well-being, in principle, takes precedence over the quest for profits. A changemaker can be an individual, a collective, an organization, a social entrepreneur, a citizen's committee, an affinity group or a broad social movement, all of which have certain common interests and deploy strategies to achieve their goals. The category of changemaker identifies the main players in the field of social innovation. The main issue at stake in the field of social innovation is "social change," an expression that can take on a variety of meanings depending on the framework of interpretation (we'll come back to this later).

In addition to these changemakers or "project leaders," there is of course a whole range of professionals and organizations who support these initiatives in various ways. These are the "professions of social innovation," which can take the form of consultants, coaches, facilitators, strategic planning advisors, communications managers, impact investors, philanthropists, university researchers, design thinking experts, communities of practice and so on.[21] The institutionalization of the field of social innovation is thus accompanied by a professionalization of the field via the introduction of rules, standards, practices, vocabularies, training, tools and devices that players are gradually learning to wield to orient themselves in this field and carry out their projects.

To mobilize resources and achieve their objectives, changemakers necessarily need to develop collaborative attitudes and social abilities (social skills) that enable them to read other players in the field, frame their discourse and actions and mobilize people in the service of certain common objectives, values or worldviews. It is indeed collective action, collaboration, resonance and mobilization capacities that are at the heart of processes aimed at meeting social needs and/or participating in social change.

But there are also dynamics of competition and multiple strategic issues linked to access to resources to carry out projects, including the search for legitimacy within the field. A changemaker will often be granted or refused certain resources or opportunities depending on the legitimacy given to them by the other players they seek to persuade or mobilize. This legitimacy is necessarily complex and situational; it may come from the field of social innovation itself but also from related fields: activist legitimacy (ideological credibility, linked to radicalism or critical sincerity), entrepreneurial legitimacy (ability to demonstrate the success of one's project in relation to market criteria), institutional legitimacy (ability to be recognized by public authorities to show that one's project effectively responds to a well-defined social problem), to name a few.

The tensions and paradoxes faced by changemakers stem from the intersection of legitimacies differentiated according to distinct fields, with potentially contradictory logics: the field of the market economy, the field of the community groups, the field of philanthropy, the academic field. The quest for legitimacy (and therefore credibility) within the field of social innovation necessarily involves a form of struggle or competition in which several players seek to mobilize resources and gain recognition from interlocutors likely to help them realize their projects. The focus of the analysis lies not so much on the realization of the social innovation project as such (which can take infinitely varied forms) but on the strategies deployed by the players to mobilize resources, persuade other players and come out on top in this complex field.

At the mesosocial or intermediary level, the field of social innovation comprises all the organizations, funding sources, governance units, values, discourses and interpretive frameworks that make it possible to draw the field's boundaries. Despite the diverse origins of changemakers, who may come from academic, political, economic, artistic, community or other backgrounds, internal governance units help to create a certain homogeneity within the field. Both dominant players and outsiders learn to familiarize themselves with a common vocabulary, understand the expectations of other players in the field and employ similar strategies. A mixture of competition and cooperation is the rule, although benevolence, collaboration, innovation and the ideal of social change are shared values. Finally, on a macrosocial scale, an analysis of the trajectories linked to the transformations and contradictions of contemporary capitalism helps to situate the genesis of the field of social innovation, like the triple movement identified earlier (commodification, social protection, emancipation). This way, we could understand the complex interactions between the paradoxes and strategic issues linked to several social effects and the internal dynamics related to the acquisition of capital, legitimacy and resonance at the microsocial level.

In the end, despite the different visions and interpretative frameworks that coexist in the field of social innovation, all the actors and organizations mentioned in this chapter collaborate, forge partnerships, exchange services, compete for grants and participate in networking events where mutual aid and self-interest are inextricably intertwined. Project leaders, funders, consultants and activist researchers interact in an arena where strategies for accumulating economic and symbolic capital, quests for legitimacy, territorial rivalries and struggles, but also sincere friendships, shared concerns for the future of the world and concern for social justice intersect.

This nuanced assessment of the world of social innovation should not be seen as a conclusion but rather as a starting point for future research into social innovation as a field. Here, we would like to support the hypothesis, which will need to be corroborated by future empirical studies, that social innovation constitutes a battlefield where the dominant players from the point of view of material resources are represented by foundations, the private impact investment sector and the state.

The convergence of the fields of social entrepreneurship, social economy and activism within the emerging field of social innovation, which has been rapidly institutionalizing since the 2010s, brings with it its share of ambiguities, novel encounters and tensions that deserve to be explored in greater detail. By delving deeper into the strategic dimensions of social innovation or by attempting to draw an ideological portrait of this shifting landscape, we hope to contribute to the questioning of the specific features of social innovation that make it so rich, without neglecting its blind spots. We need to see the complex cohabitation between competition and cooperation, interest and resonance, social impact and the unintended consequences of good intentions.

If "social innovation" is not just a buzzword but the name of a specific field defined by values, rules, norms, practices, devices, organizations and discourses, we have yet to deploy a genuine investigation of these multiple dimensions to map out the paths to emancipation. The perspective of change as a social struggle, rather than as a simple process of concertation or innovation with positive impacts on society, represents an avenue to be pursued, all the more so as social struggles are already taking place in the very arena of social innovation. If social innovation is indeed a field, then it is also a battlefield over its own meaning, foundations, struggles and aspirations.

3

Understanding the world to change it

In 2023, the richest chief executive officers in Canada earned 210 times more than the average worker: around CAD$13.2 million per year.¹ At the same time, for the great majority, wages have not kept up with inflation, and the purchasing power of Canadian families has plummeted in recent years due to rising inflation, increasing the costs of everything including food, shelter and transportation.² The poverty rate of racialized people is three times higher than that of White people. One in five Indigenous people live in poverty, as do 60 percent of Indigenous children living on reserves.³ Indigenous and Black people are also disproportionately targeted by the carceral system: the number of Indigenous people in prison has increased by 47.4 percent since 2005, while the number of Black, Asian and Spanish-speaking people has risen by 75 percent.⁴ Indigenous people now account for 28 percent of the federal prison population, despite representing only 5 percent of the overall population, and Black people makeup 9.2 percent of federally incarcerated people, more than double the 4 percent of Black people within the overall population of Canada.⁵ One in four homeless people identify as 2SLGBTQIA+,⁶ and one in six children live in a household with food insecurity.⁷ These are several examples of blatant social problems that merit a deeper analysis.

Social innovation, if it is genuinely to innovate and change things, must first try to understand the social reality it is trying to transform. This involves not only observing what is going on in the world and responding to the emergency of the moment with a creative, innovative solution but also looking beyond to the root causes of social problems and asking *why*. Where do social inequalities come from? More fundamentally, how are social problems defined in the first place? Why does environmental destruction continue even though the vast majority of people are already aware of the ecological crisis? If we cannot identify the deeper causes of social problems, we won't be able to address them with effective solutions.

Good intentions, charity and philanthropy are not enough when it comes to developing innovative solutions: we must adopt a social justice-oriented approach and stimulate our thinking from a solid, critical perspective. While the charity-based model of solidarity acts on individual and community levels, targets immediate needs and promotes acts of generosity, liberatory social innovation aims at systemic and institutional change. It takes aim at the deep causes of problems and perceives collective rights and responsibilities as instruments of a broader social equality. We *give* charity, but we *demand* social justice.

There is a marked difference between the desire to alleviate a problem and the desire to bring about a liberatory transformation of society. Of course, this does not mean that we should neglect concrete solutions to the urgent needs of the present in favor of a promised future revolution. But it is obvious that responses to social challenges will differ depending on whether our approach is based on charity or social transformation. In terms of inequalities in the food system, for example, critical food geographer Kristin Reynolds sees a difference between reducing the symptoms of injustice by promoting better access to sufficient, quality food and challenging the political and social structures underlying this injustice.[8]

Whether a particular issue is recognized as a social or individual problem is a key factor in the kinds of solutions that are proposed. Wayne Antony, publisher and writer, and sociologist Les Samuelson define social problems as "behaviors and conditions that both (objectively) harm a significant group of people and behaviors and conditions that are (subjectively) defined as harmful to a significant group of people."[9] For instance, if we look at the rates of missing and murdered Indigenous women, girls and two-spirit peoples in Canada, for many years it was largely dismissed as an individual problem, the result of poor choices by those individuals stemming from years of tragic life circumstances. In 2014, Stephen Harper, then prime minister of Canada, rejected calls for a National Inquiry, claiming these cases of missing and murdered Indigenous women were "crimes" not a "sociological phenomenon."[10] The subtext here is clear: this is not a societal problem, this is an individual problem. Thankfully, there is now widespread recognition that this is in fact a societal problem, one that requires a lens of social justice to address the root causes and systemic injustices. More recently, tensions erupted when police reported that the remains of three Indigenous women, Morgan Harris, Marcedes Myran and Rebecca Contois, were likely located in a landfill just north of Winnipeg, and the provincial government of Manitoba refused to search the landfill to recover their bodies. While the Manitoba premier tried to frame the issue as an individual, personal tragedy, one that couldn't justify the cost and risk involved in searching the landfill, critics argued it had to be understood in the context of historical and ongoing colonial violence against Indigenous Peoples.[11] It seems the people of Manitoba agreed: the government was voted out a few months later.

What is social justice?

The definition of social justice is, of course, subject to much debate, but we can say that it generally aims at social cooperation, equity and the practical conditions for the satisfaction of everyone's needs and self-fulfillment. As Janine Brodie argues, "[s]ocial justice is not a stable state to be achieved, but instead is a way of thinking and governing that prioritizes the elusive and shifting goals of fairness, equality, and inclusion."[12] This involves taking into account the specific conditions of each person and social group affected, beyond simple, abstract equality. For instance, social justice for a Black man in the United States in the 18th century, during the time of enslavement, would be different from that for a White woman in the 1960s, as it would be different for an Indigenous community in Guatemala in the 1980s.

Further, we can differentiate between notions of abstract equality, which seeks to give everyone an equivalent quantity of resources; equity, which seeks to correct inequalities for particular groups; and emancipation, which seeks to remove the barriers

Figure 3.1: Equality, equity and liberation

Note: This image has a fascinating history, having been adapted and reimagined by many organizations and artists. See Froehle, 2016.

Source: Center for Story-based Strategy and Interaction Institute for Social Change, nd. Artist: Angus Maguire, madewithangus.com (available under a Creative Commons Noncommercial Sharealike 4.0 license).

that reproduce those inequalities. The graphic in Figure 3.1 helps to illustrate some of the nuances and differences between applications of these terms.

There is a close and dynamic relationship between social justice and social innovation. Social justice asks us to consider the ends or ultimate purpose of social innovation. What is the overall vision we are seeking to achieve in implementing a particular social innovation? Without a strong normative grounding, social innovation tools and practices run the risk of perpetuating systems and structures of injustice rather than moving us toward liberation. Social innovation generally speaks to the process of social change, while social justice speaks to the end goals we seek to achieve. For example, if we look at housing, social justice helps us to name particular principles and end goals: ending homelessness, the right to housing, affordable housing. Social innovation, then, offers tools and processes through which to achieve those goals: establishing a housing cooperative, building a coalition to demand greater public investments in housing, creating a matching program pairing seniors with low-income students.

In our view, social justice should not be seen as a strict application of abstract principles, nor as a linear process in the great march of progress, but as a complex process involving advances, resistance, derailment, opposition and reversals.[13] We must take into account not only the needs of each person but the general structures and complex social relations that prevent them from leading autonomous lives.

Instead of adopting a general theory, we can more usefully identify the multiple dimensions of social justice. Feminist philosopher Nancy Fraser's work draws our attention to redistribution and recognition. In her view, redistribution is concerned with material inequality, financial imbalances between social classes, economic precarity and poverty, while problems of recognition stem from hierarchies associated with social status and diverse forms of exclusion linked to cultural representations.[14] There are also injustices of representation: Who holds decision-making power? Which voices are heard?

At first glance, this appears relatively simple, but there is often some confusion about how these questions are treated publicly. For example, economic struggles (connected to labor or to redistribution of wealth) are regularly contrasted with identity struggles (relating to marginalized groups such as women, racialized people or queer people). However, as Fraser notes, this perpetuates a false dichotomy. There are almost always redistributive *and* recognition-related aspects to any form of injustice: "Social justice today requires both redistribution and recognition. Neither alone is sufficient."[15]

Take marriage equality. At first, it seems a clear issue of recognition, seeking to grant same-sex couples the same rights and societal validation provided to heterosexual couples. And yet, it also involves economic issues of redistribution: the ability to access a partner's pension, social benefits, tax benefits, employment benefits, for example. The struggle for gender equity also involves demands for recognition and redistribution. Women are paid less compared to men, earning CAD$0.87 for every dollar earned by their male counterparts in Canada in 2022. The gap is even larger when looking at racialized and Indigenous women.[16] Women also experience drastically higher rates of harassment and sexual violence compared to men, with women five times more likely to be sexually assaulted than men – and women with a disability four times more likely to be sexually assaulted than women without a disability. As the #MeToo movement helped to highlight, struggles for recognition and redistribution are deeply intertwined, and meaningful progress requires attention to both.

Other mobilizations, seemingly belonging to the economic sphere, can also have roots in identity politics. For instance, the yellow vest movement in France formed in opposition to the increased taxation of gas and decreased purchasing power. However, it also erupted in part from a sense of moral indignation against political elites who seemingly lacked sympathy for their situation, making statements such as: "There are those who succeed, and those who are nothing."[17]

Confronted with these different forms of injustice, Fraser proposes that we think about social justice through the lens of "parity of participation." This principle requires that each person has the ability to partake equally in social and political interactions, which necessitates both redistribution and mutual recognition. In short, everyone must have access to certain material conditions to satisfy their needs, and everyone must also be able to obtain a certain degree of recognition to feel respected and considered a full person. However, how these principles are put into practice remains a source of tension and discussion. Who is empowered to bestow recognition – who recognizes and who is recognized? Indigenous scholars Glen Coulthard and Audra Simpson offer important critiques on the limits of recognition, noting that while a liberal politics of recognition may offer additional economic or social rights, it maintains a fundamentally unjust system. Speaking to the Canadian government's supposed efforts at reconciliation with Indigenous Peoples, Coulthard notes:

> Instead of ushering in an era of peaceful coexistence grounded on the ideal of reciprocity or mutual recognition, the politics of recognition in its contemporary liberal form promises to reproduce the very configurations of colonialist, racist, patriarchal state power that Indigenous peoples' demands for recognition have historically sought to transcend.[18]

Instead, Coulthard sees potential and possibility in an Indigenous resurgence, emphasizing the rebuilding and strengthening of

Indigenous culture, political systems and knowledge as opposed to seeking recognition from the state. He sees this as a path not only to resist capitalism but to provide alternatives through Indigenous social, political and economic experimentation.

As we shall see in Chapter 5, adopting an intersectional lens is one way we can ensure struggles for recognition and redistribution move us toward social transformation.

Environmental justice

Given the increasing recognition of the climate catastrophe, as well as the importance of nonhuman animals, biodiversity and ecosystem health to visions of equality and liberation, environmental justice has become a driving force for many social innovation initiatives. While some would conceptualize environmental justice as a component of social justice, we find it useful to position it as a complementary and parallel concept. Environmental justice is undoubtedly connected to social justice, as environmental issues have social consequences, just as social issues have environmental consequences, and environmental justice is a product of the same systems and structures of oppression that produce and reproduce social injustices.

Environmental justice responds to the unequal distribution of environmental risks and benefits within society, as well as the exclusion of marginalized groups from the governance and management of the environment. An important insight from environmental justice is the phenomenon of environmental racism. First coined by US civil rights activist Benjamin Chavis, it highlights the ways racialized and Indigenous communities have been disproportionately subjected to environmental harms and deliberately targeted by governments and corporate entities for the disposal of toxic waste and other environmental pollutants. For example, environmental racism helps us to understand the root causes of long-term boil water advisories on multiple Indigenous reserves in Canada or the placement of waste disposal sites and other toxic industries in close proximity to historically Black and Indigenous communities in Nova Scotia.[19] It also calls into question the framing of "natural" disasters, turning our attention to the fact that those countries that have predominantly caused climate change are not the same countries most impacted.[20]

But social innovation can't stop at moral reflection if it intends to change the world and have a real impact. On top of the desire for social justice, a critical understanding of the world is needed. This involves looking at social problems as manifestations of power relations rather than individual problems, poor choices or simply bad luck. While it can be very important to take the individual and psychological dimensions of everyday problems into account, the root structural social causes must not be ignored.

The art of prefiguration

After coming to understand "why" there are injustices and "how" they are perpetuated, we arrive at the awkward question: Now what? Faced with the enormous injustices of today's society, we often feel overwhelmed by the magnitude of the challenges that must be overcome. Unfortunately, critical reflection sometimes makes us feel powerless, making us feel that we are unable to change things or creating uncertainty about where to start.

To keep fatalism at bay, we must find ways of combining awareness-raising and the desire for change, searching for truth and building the power to act. Too many critical analyses leave no place for alternatives, few possibilities for transformation and create contradictions that could reverse the situation. Conversely, the attitude of positive thinking at all costs (toxic positivity), which tends to ignore critiques, negativity and conflict to focus on solutions and success stories and celebrate other local initiatives, too often fails to see the limits to solutions as well as the barriers to their future development. What we need is a balance between critical thinking and openness to possibilities. Chris Dixon, social movement scholar, and Alexis Shotwell, social and political theorist, draw on Antonio Gramsci to describe a "grieving optimism" as a productive orientation to organizing in the context of the climate crisis:

> Perhaps we can be grieving optimists. We can have what Italian communist Antonio Gramsci popularized as "pessimism of the intellect, optimism of the will."

> Pessimism of the intellect means having the courage to confront the world realistically and take worst-case scenarios seriously. Organizing out of our grief for this planet and all of us on it rests on the certain knowledge that, for the vast majority of us who are not rich, most of the problems facing us now are at a scale beyond our individual capacity to solve. The way to be a grieving optimist is to band together with others who care about this world, and to struggle.[21]

This grieving optimism calls on us to meet our challenges head-on, not to shy away from the full scope of the crisis (be it climate, drug overdoses or racialized police violence) but to use that shared recognition as a source of collective power and strength rather than a reason to not take action.

Liberatory social innovation, for this reason, assumes a "politics of possibility." According to feminist geographers J.K. Gibson-Graham, such a politics aims to create a new political imaginary, to develop a new language that broadens our understanding of economic processes, to stimulate ethical thinking about diverse ways of organizing society and to experiment with new forms of living.[22] Economically, we can imagine diverse ways of producing, exchanging and consuming that go beyond a "capital-centric" vision of the world that views private enterprise, the market, wage labor and the drive to maximize profit as the sole possible horizon.

For example, we can shift our gaze away from the dominant forms of the economy and observe a multiplicity of economic practices currently existing in the world. As we will see in Chapter 8, there are already many different economic rationalities at play coexisting with, and alongside, capitalist logic, like the proverbial iceberg whose submerged mass contains a host of practices based on principles of mutual aid, cooperation, donation and solidarity.[23]

We can apply the same logic to diverse social practices that do not conform to heterosexist, racist, colonial hierarchies. This is not a matter of ignoring structures of oppression and simply celebrating alternatives but a matter of striving, in the present, to cultivate and encourage other ways of living, organizing, producing and relating to others despite those structures of harm and destruction. As poet Paul Éluard said: "Another world is possible, and it is within this one."[24]

This brings us to the idea of cultivating a "radical imagination"[25] and the need to "decolonize our imaginary"[26] to think of new institutions and forms of life beyond the established order. We can thus speak of a "prefigurative politics" that aims to embody in the present the ways of being that we would like to see on a large scale in a future society.[27] It is a matter of collapsing the distance between the ideal and reality, between the world not yet arrived and present possibilities. Erik Olin Wright uses the expression "real utopias"[28] to designate desirable, viable and realizable alternatives in the current world, such as self-managed cooperatives, the commons, community land trusts and so on.[29]

The field of social innovation should thus be understood as a space of convergence between utopia and pragmatism, imagination and rigorous social analysis, creativity and strategy. Of course, there are a host of conflicts between the world as it is and the world as we would like it to be, between possibilities inscribed in the interstices of current society and the difficulties of organizing to bring about the desired change. This is why, as political philosopher Angela Davis emphasizes, freedom must be understood as a *constant struggle* to combine individual will and collective action to bring about a practical transformation of the world.[30]

4

The past as possibilities

Creating a new political imaginary and possibilities beyond the world we live in implies a critical understanding of the social reality to be transformed. As the previous chapter clearly shows, radical imagination, transformative and prefigurative projects and possible alternatives depend on a careful appreciation of social problems and what creates and sustains them. With this in mind, and rightly so, one of the first avenues to be explored if we are to understand the structuring of today's world will undoubtedly be to look at the world of yesterday. In asking what fuels the environmental crisis in the 21st century, for example, we will also need to ask ourselves how and when, in the past decades and centuries, we got to the point of destroying the environment. In trying to understand the parameters of today's housing crises, we must look into the emergence of the mode of production that transforms a roof into a commodity. Similarly, to understand racism and heterosexism as structural and social issues that go beyond individual attitudes, we must look at the development of these ideas in the history of European modernity.

To gain a critical understanding of the world as we know it, in other words, we must turn to the past, which informs us about the roots of the social problems we identify and enables us to grasp more accurately both the structures that support them and how to dismantle those structures. As philosopher Alia Al-Saji suggests about colonial and racial issues, "[c]olonial and racial formations endure and are rephrased – or, more precisely, in enduring are rephrased, without losing hold."[1] That said, examining the past also comes with certain risks and limits that must be guarded against, if we are to preserve the richness of what the past offers us, and what it enables us to do in the present.

If the past reveals the depths of what needs to be repaired, its weight can lead to a certain fatalism. How can we end a practice so deeply rooted in history? How long will it take to transform an institution or structure that has been perfected over the ages? The hold of the past can certainly be discouraging, and it can create the feeling that transformations and innovations are unattainable. This is all the more true when we consider the extent of the strategies deployed to hinder and render obsolete past hopes and alternatives, from the production of oblivion and erasure of emancipatory struggles and movements to contemporary recuperations of past radical innovations and transformations.

Conversely, historicizing can also lead to confusing critical understanding and effective transformation. As queer scholar Eve Sedgwick warns us, the relationship to the past in critical thought often tends to confuse the discovery of the depth of violence with its end, "as though to make something visible as a problem was, if not a mere hop, skip, and jump from getting it solved, at least self-evidently a step in that direction."[2] Unfortunately, as we know, a detailed understanding of the various problems we face – from growing inequalities to the environmental crisis, from sexist and transphobic violence to racism and xenophobia – is not enough to put an end to them.

While the past informs our critical reading of the world, if we intend to transform our world, it is crucial to distill the past in a way that allows rather than prevents, so that the hold does not hold. To do this, we need to consider the past not only as the accumulation that makes up the present – that is, the texture of the problems we have to deal with today – but also as a repertoire of what was different, what was not yet or not quite and what could have been possible. Transforming implies believing that things can be better. There is, therefore, necessarily a temporal humility, an awareness of the inadequacies of a present that is not enough. This same understanding must apply to the past: "Because the reader has room to realize that the future may be different from the present, it is also possible for her to entertain such profoundly painful, profoundly relieving, ethically crucial possibilities as that the past, in turn, could have happened differently from the way it actually did."[3] Looking at the past, in other words, not only enables us to diagnose but also opens up possibilities for venturing into the otherwise.

Beyond revealing the texture of present problems, the past can inform at least three ways of transforming the present. First, it tells us what was different before, outside or against what we want to change. Second, it informs us about what has been hoped for and attempted against the various developments our present moment inherits. And finally, it invites us to imagine what might not have survived the passage of time but could have existed and could have been hoped for and attempted. Of course, these three categories of the past are not rigidly distinguishable. Specific democratic experiments, for example, or certain revolutions, lie on their porous borders: they existed in part but not entirely or not long enough to unfold fully, or we know only certain aspects of them, which means that while they existed in part, they also remained anticipations and are not fully known and knowable. Despite this porosity, however, sticking schematically to these three distinct forms of transformative sources nevertheless allows us to distinguish three operations for mobilizing the past for what it does as well as for what it could do: (a) the resurgence and regeneration of what has been different in a present that is past; (b) the restaging of past possibilities, or what the *not yet* and *not quite* have promised in the past; and (c) the imagining of what could have been.

Resurgence and regeneration

The world we want to change did not always exist and has not always existed everywhere. Like the present, the past is full of ways of living together according to entirely different parameters and scales. Of course, what once existed cannot be considered a ready-made model to be reproduced today, regardless of context. Just as future possibilities depend on a solid understanding of the present, the transformative and innovative utility of what once existed depends on its recontextualization. It is this mediation between the past and its contextual adaptation that critical Indigenous perspectives envisage, in a remarkably useful way, as the process of resurgence and regeneration. Kanien'kehá:ka (Mohawk) thinker

Taiaiake Alfred, in particular, has devoted much thought to the possibilities afforded by this very mediation.

To dwell on the transformative possibilities of what has existed, Alfred develops a theory of change centering on a regenerative gesture. This involves not only turning away, rejecting and refusing the violence of past and present colonization but also insisting on the contextual adaptation of Indigenous traditions, that is, their "regeneration":

> The sovereignty movement is now characterized by efforts to re-construct the elements of nationhood rather than to develop the means for further integrating Natives into the institutions of the dominant society. Relying on indigenous values and principles and on unique conceptions of key terms in the debate, many Native communities have embarked on a radically different path than the integrative processes represented by claims for self-government or aboriginal rights.[4]

The operation put forth by Alfred suggests exploring the mediation between tradition and its re-creation as well as the many possibilities and openings allowed by the latter in the specific context of his community of Kahnawà:ke and, more broadly, for an Onkwehonwe (Indigenous) theory of change. Alfred develops different terms for this: in *Heeding the Voices of Our Ancestors: Kahnawake Mohawk Politics and the Rise of Native Nationalism* (1995), he refers to the "Adaptiveness of Tradition," while the term mobilized in *Wasáse: Indigenous Pathways of Action and Freedom* (2009) is "regeneration." Both allow us to understand the rejection of the inadequacies of the present as the elaboration of "new and creative ways to express that heritage,"[5] and it is in the process of this elaboration that Alfred situates the openness to different elements that can intervene and be integrated into "adaptiveness" or "regeneration," that is, different contextual, pragmatic, endogenous or exogenous elements, which will co-constitute the new arrangements that "adaptiveness" or "regeneration" sets in motion.

Alfred builds this approach on the experience of his community. In 1995, he first developed the idea of an "Adaptiveness of Tradition" that would be distinctive and specific to the Kahnawa'keró:non (people of Kahnawà:ke). Their political identity, Alfred tells us, is rooted precisely in this effort to mediate between tradition and change and between political proximity and distance in relation to the Iroquois Confederacy of which they are a part:

> The Mohawks of Kahnawake inherited the rich legacy of the Mohawk Nation and the Iroquois Confederacy. But they are also descended from a group of people who rejected the political constraints of that tradition to stake out their own distinct place between the native society and the new European society.[6]

While in the community's recent history, traditional Iroquois structures and values have emerged as the appropriate framework for considering self-determination, he points out that "the need to root novel responses in the familiar ground of traditional Iroquois values is its most constant feature."[7] This rediscovered and renewed need has been expressed, Alfred continues, even more markedly since the intracommunity discussions on the protection of lands and rights of the first half of the 20th century: "In a sense, re-creating the political ideology of the Iroquois was a natural response in searching for a means of protecting the distinctiveness and territorial integrity of their community."[8] Adaptiveness, however, is not only temporal but also contextual. It necessarily implies the context in which the rearticulation of tradition is envisaged. In this sense, Alfred proposes to think of adaptiveness as a form of "syncretism," understood here not just as a religious phenomenon but as a political, cultural and ideological one. "Newfound elements were integrated according to a pragmatic evaluation of Mohawk interests and needs."[9]

Kahnawà:ke activist Louis Karoniaktajeh Hall's perspectives on the Kaianere'kó:wa, or Great Law of Peace, provide a good example. Kaianere'kó:wa is the Iroquois constitution drawn up centuries ago on the initiative of Deganawida, founder of the Iroquois Confederacy. It establishes a participatory and consensual democracy as well as common and reciprocal sovereignty and, to this end, contains 117 articles detailing the rights and duties of lords, election processes, clans and forms of membership, international rules, warfare and human rights. In Karoniaktajeh's reading of the tradition, Kaianere'kó:wa appears as the ideal and just form of governance but also as a malleable heritage that is necessarily open to revision: "In Louis Hall's work, the Gayanerekowa [Kaianere'kó:wa] is treated as a just and desirable model for governance, but one that may be revised and transformed according to its own democratic principles, rather than procedure."[10] It is not a matter of directly translating the past into the present but of a critical mediation. As activist Ellen Gabriel, a well-known figure of Kahnawà:ke's sister community of Kanehsatà:ke, similarly suggests:

> It is supposed to adapt to the times that people are living in, and when we do that we are able to bring our democracy to a higher level and a different level, but still having that foundational understanding of those ancestral teachings of being kind to the earth, being respectful to the earth, leaving something – a legacy – behind.[11]

Initially thought of retrospectively from the perspective of his community, Alfred's mediation between the past and its contextual adaptation later took on a forward-looking intention and a broader Onkwehonwe scope. The Onkwehonwe resurgence that Alfred outlined more recently is envisaged as a revolutionary struggle that is at once spiritual, social and political: "A spiritual revolution, a culturally rooted social movement that transforms the whole of society and a political action that seeks to remake the entire landscape of power and relationship to reflect truly a liberated post-imperial vision."[12] It is in this perspective of a transformative cultural and traditional anchorage that regeneration appears as the central element of Onkwehonwe resurgence. In line with what Alfred earlier referred to as the "Adaptiveness of Tradition," regeneration is a creative and contextual reworking of tradition:

> Regeneration means we will reference ourselves differently, both from the ways we did traditionally and under colonial domination. We will self-consciously

recreate our cultural practices and reform our political identities by drawing on tradition in a thoughtful process of reconstruction and a committed reorganization of our lives in a personal and collective sense.[13]

But while Alfred, at first, retrospectively documented syncretism in the Kahnawà:ke political experience – that is, openness to different elements that can intervene and be integrated into Kanien'kehá:ka – starting in the mid-2000s, the intervention of exogenous factors in the Onkwehonwe regeneration process was then presented as an invitation: "The non-indigenous will be shown a new path and offered the chance to join in a renewed relationship between the peoples and places of this land, which we occupy together."[14] Resurgence, Alfred tells us, is thus a common, pan-Indigenous struggle and, at the same time, a broader invitation to decolonial coexistence.

As critical Indigenous perspectives on resurgence and regeneration suggest, what has been can be mobilized for transformation and innovation on a local, regional and even continental scale through a critical mediation that is attentive to context and remains open to the various new elements that may come into play. This process, moreover, can be envisaged not only in relation to ancestral traditions but also to different forms of organizing and activism. This is what, for example, scholar Michael Hardt suggests when looking at the subversion and liberation movements that took shape in the 1970s: "They offer us, in other words, not only initial analyses of today's structures of economic and political domination, and not only effective forms of critique and resistance against them, but also experiments with alternative social and political relations on the path to liberation."[15]

Restaging hope

Investigating the past allows for radical imagination and future possibilities based on what existed before, outside or against what our present inherits. But for the purposes of transformation and innovation, the past contains more than what existed and can be adapted in the present. It also contains a wealth of unfulfilled promises. It is also a reservoir of hopes, anticipations, imaginations and utopias that have not materialized. In other words, beyond what has existed and can be contextually adapted, the past also offers us a repertoire of past futurities, things that were not yet or not quite revealing how others before us envisioned something better than their present, which was not enough. As with what has existed, the usefulness of anticipations that did not materialize will depend on their content and contextualization in today's world. In this respect, the process is quite similar: in the same way that we can regenerate a traditional organizational form or alternative social relations, we can mobilize the political program of a party that was never elected, the archives of a social center project that never saw the light of day or a revolutionary impulse that was interrupted. But unlike the resurgence, since these promises did not materialize or did not fully materialize, it is not only their content that informs us but also their anticipatory character in the context in which they occurred. What made these rehearsals possible, and what prevented them from realization? What made these hopes real possibilities, and what interrupted them? Based on these questions, scholar Ariella Aïsha Azoulay suggests paying attention to imperialism and anti-imperialism:

> Situations described as failed moments of resistance to imperial power, the failure of which is taken as accepted fact, will be restaged differently: first, in order to retrieve a world in which this fact was not yet accomplished and the imperial condition could not be taken for granted; second in order to enable these statements and modalities of protest, erased by imperial power, to emerge again as competing valid options.[16]

Our attention will first turn to what led to the formulation of these hopes, attempts, promises or, as queer theorist José Esteban Muñoz puts it, "[a] thing that is present but not actually existing in the present tense."[17] To what specific realities did these anticipations attempt to respond? Which group(s) were behind these hopes? These are the questions, for example, that activist, agronomist and thinker Amílcar Cabral invites us to answer by looking at African liberation struggles to open up future possibilities. To fully understand these struggles' desires, hopes and strategies and to help such desires, hopes and strategies reemerge, we first need a detailed understanding of the context in which they unfolded, that is, the different forms of imperialism that gave rise to them. While the main characteristic of imperialism is the negation of the historical process of colonized peoples, Cabral distinguishes two forms of imperialism that have implied different responses:

- Direct domination – by means of a political power made up of agents foreign to the dominated people (armed forces, police, administrative agents and settlers) – which is conventionally called *classical colonialism* or *colonialism*.
- Indirect domination – by means of a political power made up mainly or completely of native agents – which is conventionally called *neocolonialism*.[18]

In Africa, Cabral tells us, direct domination has sometimes led to the partial destruction of societies, a moderate settlement by an exogenous population and, sometimes, to the geographical, economic and political confinement of Indigenous societies for the benefit of an exogenous population. Subsequent indirect domination, differently, took the form of the creation of a local bourgeoisie answering to the exogenous power. For Cabral, national liberation as anticipation consequently means the rejection, by a given socioeconomic group or ensemble, of the negation of its historical process: "The national liberation of a people is the regaining of the historical personality of that people, it is their return to history through the destruction of the imperialist domination to which they were subjected."[19] In other words, African countries have gained their independence, but national liberation anticipates a more profound structural transformation and "is not over at the moment when the flag is hoisted and the national anthem is played."[20] It thus remained (and remains) an anticipation.

However, depending on whether the context was one of direct or indirect domination, this anticipation was lodged in different groups within society. In the context of "classical" colonialism – that is, in a relatively horizontal organization of Indigenous society vis-à-vis the exogenous entity – the group bearing the liberating promises was an active minority or revolutionary vanguard: "While we admit that everyone knows best what to do in his own house, we feel that among these measures it is vital to create a firmly united vanguard, conscious of the true meaning and objective of the national liberation struggle which it must lead."[21] In the context of neocolonialism, differently, a context in which the structure of Indigenous society has become vertically complex, notably with the creation of a local bourgeoisie, Cabral locates the emancipatory impulse no longer within the vanguard but within a specific class: "This class of workers [urbanized industrial workers and agricultural proletarians], whatever the degree of development of its political consciousness (beyond a certain minimum that is *consciousness of its needs*), seems to constitute the true popular vanguard of the national liberation struggle in the neocolonial case."[22]

Once we have identified the conditions of the emergence of a past promise, desire or anticipation, its usefulness for the present will then be measured in terms of what made it something that could happen rather than something doomed not to happen. What made emancipatory hope in Africa, to stay with our example, a possibility? For this, we can draw on the different "layers of the category Possibility" distinguished by philosopher Ernst Bloch. First, the "formally Possible" refers to "something conceptually possible" that can be thought of without regard to the actual relationships between things. Second, "factually-objectively Possible" refers to what is possible in relation to what is empirically known in the present, considered "scientific or socio-historical given facts."[23] Third, "fact-based object-suited Possible" designates what is possible not only in terms of what we know about a thing but what that thing itself can become outside our present knowledge. Finally, the "objectively-real Possible" designates what is possible not only in the thing itself but in its relation to the "unexhausted whole of the world itself."[24]

However, understanding a possibility as "objectively-real" does not change the fact that it has not come true. In the last instance, the past can tell us what prevented its realization. What held back emancipatory hope? Whereas the previous questions enabled us to identify what made past hopes possible and what made them real possibilities so that they can be restaged according to their contextual adaptation, this last question enables us to use the past preventively. Of course, as their emergence or the test of their possibility might tell us, some of the reasons different hopes were not realized can be found in their formulation. But the past also informs us of the exogenous elements that obstructed the passage from anticipation to realization. If we return one last time to the example of African liberation struggles, a series of retrospective questions allows us to plan more adequately for the future. What was the impact, for instance, of different colonial and neocolonial counterinsurgency tactics? How can we measure the effect of technological disparities? What role did international cooperation, nongovernmental organizations and supra-state institutions play? Which new players have entered the scene? If we wish to restage past hopes and anticipations, a good understanding of what made them impossible will enable us to better preserve the possibilities they offer us in the present.

From what could have been (hoped for) to what could be

We now have some guidelines for working with what comes to us from the past. Whether we are talking about what once existed or what was envisioned, the transformative sources we have recovered so far come from the various artifacts we have access to. But what about what the archives and testimonies of the past have wholly erased, have not saved? If we want to transform the world toward social justice, can our view of the past be restricted to what the rich, the White, the male and the cisheterosexual have written and preserved, or even to what has managed to make its way to us against all odds? Is there not, possibly, a past that does not reach us precisely because of what we want to break from? Since history, understood as a specific organization of the past, does not tell us everything, the past calls not only for resurgence and restaging but also for imagination. As poet M. NourbeSe Philip urges us: "There is no telling this story: it must be told."[25]

This process, which involves accepting and going beyond the limits of the archive to establish a relationship with a past that might have been, is what literary scholar and cultural historian Saidiya Hartman calls "critical fabulation."[26] Attending to the archives of slavery, which are archives produced by the masters, Hartman reminds us that their limits prevent us from knowing precisely what has been different and what has been hoped for and attempted. In other words, everything that exceeded slavery's violence can only exist in the present in the register of the speculative. But that does not mean we should not be attentive to it. On the contrary, this speculative past informs us in itself, and to attend to it, Hartman proposes a method that refuses both the authority of what is given as legible in the dominant narrative and the temptation to fill factual or objective voids, a method for imagining, instead, in the space of the conditional:

> Is it possible to exceed or negotiate the constitutive limits of the archive? By advancing a series of speculative arguments and exploiting the capacities of the subjunctive (a grammatical mood that expresses doubts, wishes, and possibilities), in fashioning a narrative, which is based upon archival research, and by that I mean a critical reading of the archive that mimes the figurative dimensions of history, I intended both to tell an impossible story and to amplify the impossibility of its telling.[27]

Critical fabulation blurs the distinction between proven and unproven, possible and impossible, stable and unstable. The conditional that enables it inscribes not only this or that element of the past in our present but even more so the past itself in the space of what must be refashioned, alongside the present and the future. It is not, therefore, a question of finding what the archive renders absent but of forcing the archive's limit, of engaging with its impossibility to see openings in it so its hold does not hold. With and against archives such as fugitive slave advertisements, notarial deeds, newspaper clippings, constitutional laws, slave ship ledgers, letters, maps, land registration, criminal and medical records and so on, it thus becomes possible to imagine practices of resistance, forms of collective decision making or hopes that could have been and that can still feed the present regardless of their validity according to historical methods.

What once existed can reemerge, what was hoped for can be restaged and what could have been (hoped for) can be imagined. Whether verified, anticipatory or speculative, the past, perhaps more than anything else, invites us to insist that there is more than what is not enough.

5

Centering intersectionality and equity

As the previous chapters made clear, students and practitioners of social innovation can greatly benefit from critical thinking and praxis that recognizes the complexity of structural oppression, careful engagement with past possibilities as well as tools and frameworks that can address the multiplicity of intersecting inequalities. In this chapter, we focus on the importance of structural oppression and the learnings we can apply to advancing equity and justice from intersectional feminism, antiracist and anti-oppression frameworks. We conclude with thoughts on transformative justice within social organizations and movements.

Understanding structures of oppression

Flexing our critical thinking skills on a social problem involves three steps. As introduced in Chapter 3, first, we need to confirm if it is a social or collective problem and not simply an individual case. Second, we must clarify the underlying causes, social actors, practices and structures that are at the root of the problem while also accounting for the social, political, cultural and historical contexts. Third, we identify and develop solutions to overcome the problem – that is, how we can sustainably transform the situation based on the needs of the collective.

To identify the structural causes at the root of social problems, we must study the complex relations between social structures, institutions, social groups and individuals. As sociologist C. Wright Mills highlights, from a sociological point of view, an individual's life and the history of society cannot be understood in isolation from each other. Using our sociological imagination involves identifying the different forms of domination, and thus the systems of oppression and privileges, that reproduce structural inequalities between social groups. Privilege and oppression are relational, interconnected and interdependent (see Figure 5.1).

We will start by clarifying some terms that are often misunderstood. *Oppression* refers to a systematic process of disadvantaging a group of people because they belong to a social category defined by their class, gender, sexuality, ethnicity, religion, race, disability and so on. Manifestations of oppression are generally normalized in society, which means they seem natural or are taken for granted. Dominant groups are privileged

Figure 5.1: The wheel of power and privilege

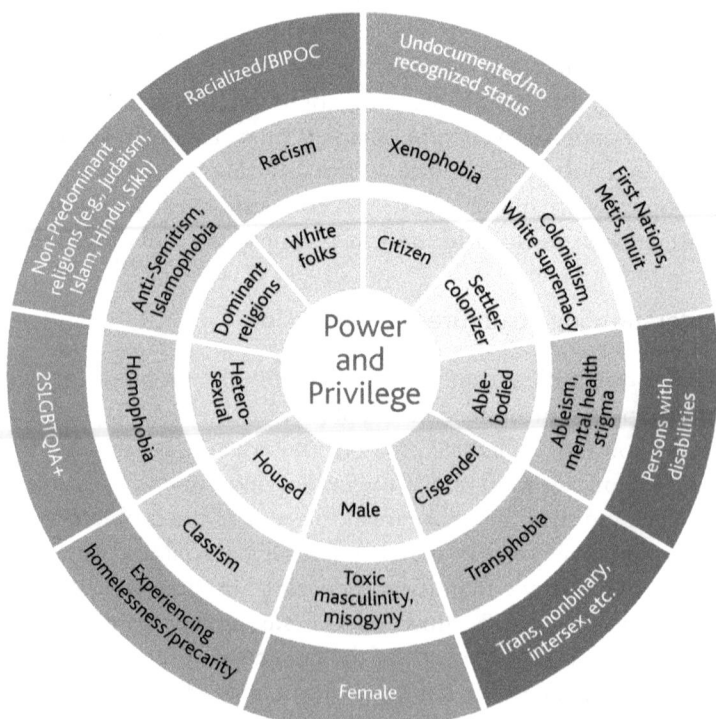

Note: BIPOC = Black Indigenous and People of Colour
Source: University of Guelph, 2022

in the sense that they have better access to material resources, opportunities, recognition, social power and cultural capital relative to disadvantaged groups. Privileged groups are advantaged by this asymmetry, often without being aware of it: "Privilege is unearned power and benefits, based on identities, status, or background variables."[1]

Power, on the other hand, refers to an individual's capacity to influence, shape or control a direction or outcome in relation to the experiences and actions or thoughts and feelings of individuals or groups. Power dynamics play a central role in oppressive systems, where certain individuals or groups hold more power than others, leading to inequalities, marginalization and discrimination. Power is relational, dynamic and contextual. It can be enacted at various levels – individual, institutional, structural, cultural and social. In their book *Intersectionality*, Patricia Hill Collins and Sirma Bilge refer to various "domains of power": structural, disciplinary, cultural and interpersonal.[2] Power can be materially based (economic), but it can also derive from status (authority, custom) and cultural capital (intangible assets, skills, education, knowledge).

Relations of oppression are not simply unequal interpersonal relationships between individuals, where each can change their position at will. Nor are they the result of a simple social stratification, as though society were a giant mille-feuille where individuals of various classes could change their condition with a good education system and strong social mobility. Systems of oppression are unequal social relations between antagonistic interests that are formed into lasting structures, such as capitalism, heteropatriarchy and colonialism.

Intersectionality

We can observe the complex interweaving of these various forms of oppression through an intersectional perspective and critically analyze the complexity of identity and people's intersecting experiences. This allows us to understand how social relations of power – based on race, gender, class, age, ability, sexuality and so on – intersect and shape one another to produce unique social inequalities and experiences with an understanding of power relations at its core. As Sumi Cho, legal scholar known for her contributions to critical race theory and intersectionality, and colleagues explain: "Intersectionality is an analytic disposition … what makes an analysis intersectional – whatever terms it deploys, whatever its iteration, whatever its field or discipline – is its adoption of an intersectional way of thinking about the problem of sameness and difference and its relation to power."[3]

Since the 1970s, in response to White liberal feminism, which dominated the women's movement and academic spaces, Black feminist and critical race scholars and activists (such as bell hooks, Angela Davis, Frances Beale and Toni Cade Bambara) challenged liberal, White, heterosexual, middle-class conceptualizations of women's experiences of patriarchy, sexism and misogyny. Instead, they advocated for a more complex, layered and nuanced understanding of how gender, race and class create different and unique experiences of oppression, marginalization and discrimination as well as access to opportunity, power, influence and resources. Indeed, as civil rights activist Audre Lorde powerfully stated in 1982: "There is no such thing as a single-issue struggle because we do not live single-issue lives."

These critiques and insights were greatly influenced by grassroots Black feminist movements and activism. The Combahee River Collective Statement is widely recognized as one of the foundational feminist intersectional texts that recognized how systems of power related to race, gender and class are interconnected:

> We are actively committed to struggling against racial, sexual, heterosexual, and class oppression, and see as our particular task the development of integrated analysis and practice based upon the fact that the major systems of oppression are interlocking. The synthesis of these oppressions creates the conditions of our lives. As Black women we see Black feminism as the logical political movement to combat the manifold and simultaneous oppressions that all women of color face.[4]

Building on Black feminist traditions, which critique how race and racism are embedded in social structures, intersectionality became a powerful mechanism to recognize and analyze intersecting forms of oppression and disadvantage (see Figure 5.2). Kimberlé Crenshaw, prominent legal scholar and Executive Director of the African American Policy Forum, first coined the term "intersectionality" in 1989 as a theoretical concept to demonstrate how different forms of discrimination, such as racism, heterosexism, homophobia, transphobia and classism, are interconnected and mutually reinforcing. Crenshaw developed the theory of intersectionality to explain the double discrimination of racism *and* sexism that Black women experience through her research of employment discrimination in the legal case *DeGraffenreid v. General Motors*. In the 1976 case, Black female employees of General Motors claimed that they were fired due to a unique form of discrimination because they were Black and women. The court's decision against their claims reflected an inability to recognize the multiple and intersecting discriminations and treated race and gender separately.[5]

For those living at the intersection of multiple marginalized identities, these systems of oppression can create compounded disadvantages for individuals. According to Bilge and Collins, intersectionality is an "analytic sensitivity" enabling us to define the complexity of social situations starting from the intersection of power relations.[6] In other words, an individual's social location cannot be understood through a single social category nor by simply adding up the effects of each system of oppression. In reality, each experience involves multiple, overlapping power relations, often contradictory and with diverse effects.

For example, Indigenous women, girls and 2SLGBTQIA+ face multiple forms of discrimination and marginalization due to their gender and Indigenous identity. The intersection of gender and race results in significant health, social and economic disparities rooted in White supremacy, colonialism and heteropatriarchy. The National Inquiry into Missing and Murdered Indigenous Women and Girls (2019) reveals the multiple and deliberate ways that Indigenous women experience unique oppression and marginalization across various systems and institutions (cultural support, education, housing, employment, health) as serious human and Indigenous rights violations and abuses.[7] These human rights violations and abuses are at the root of the heightened levels

Figure 5.2: Feminist intersectionality poster

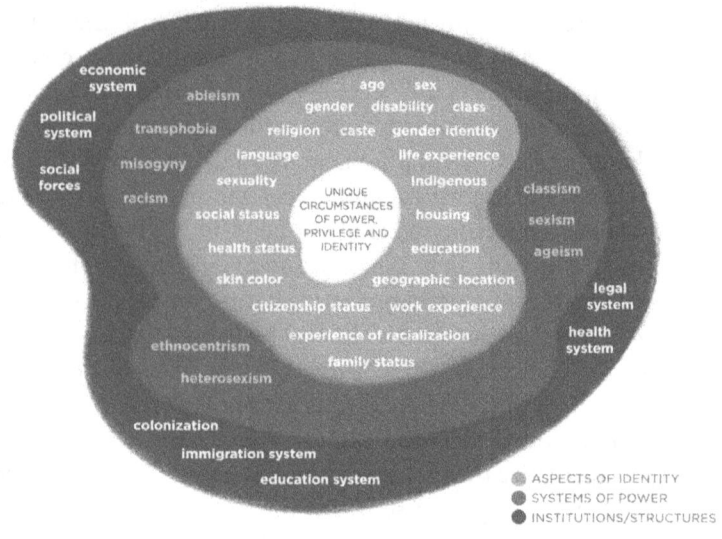

Source: Canadian Research Institute for the Advancement of Women, 2021

of violence and femicide that Indigenous women experience: they are six times more likely to be killed than non-Indigenous women in Canada.[8]

As Figure 5.2 shows, intersectionality is not merely adding layers; it's about the relationship and dynamic between the different social groupings and categories, which are socially constructed and reinforce unequal power relations between groups and individuals as well as systems.

Intersectionality and praxis: antiracism and anti-oppression

Today, intersectionality is a foundational theoretical concept and practice informing critical praxis in feminist and gender studies classrooms and social movements focused on gender justice on an international scale. However, with this recognition is the risk of cooptation, misappropriation and depoliticization – especially in relation to its Black, antiracist roots. For example, the Canadian government's application of Gender-Based Analysis Plus, an analytic tool intended to provide an intersectional gender analysis, has been widely critiqued as a "fundamental misunderstanding of intersectionality" that "runs counter to an intersectional approach" because different intersecting identities are treated as additive.[9] While an opening to include gender mainstreaming into the political discourse of Canadian politics has the potential to transform policy, a more complex and nuanced understanding of intersectionality is needed to fully integrate a GBA+ framework that can be truly transformative.

Combining intersectionality as a theory and practical applications of anti-oppression frameworks allows us to see how oppression and power operate and where an individual may experience oppression in one area yet occupy a space of privilege in another. Anti-oppression not only challenges power dynamics but also works to create space and empower those who experience oppression. Similarly, antiracism seeks to identify and recognize systemic racism and works to actively challenge, dismantle and eradicate systemic racism (such as White supremacy) in its many forms including structures, policies and practices within institutions such as schools, workplaces, criminal justice systems and social services. This often extends to various social contexts including social movements, nonprofits, collectives and community groups. Antiracism includes challenging implicit biases that perpetuate discriminatory attitudes and behaviors but also involves education to promote awareness of structural racism, policy advocacy (health care, education, criminal justice system) and acknowledging the privilege and power of the racial identities that continue to benefit from systemic racism.

Together antiracism and anti-oppression (ARAO) form a framework and set of principles that are *actively* involved in dismantling all forms of oppression and promoting social justice and equity. Using a systemic analysis of oppression and racism, ARAO challenges power imbalances, encourages inclusivity and representation (not tokenism or symbolic effort), advocates for engaged allyship to fight social injustice, promotes reflexivity and seeks opportunities for solidarity and collective action. ARAO can help transform a theoretical exercise of intersectionality into a powerful framework for resistance within classrooms, social organizations and social movement spaces.

Grassroots activists, community groups and scholars frequently apply both frameworks to understand and address the complexities of social injustice and work toward more inclusive and equitable societies. This has been particularly useful in a strategy and prerequisite for successful feminist coalitions, "which foster the representation and participation of multiply-marginalized groups."[10] For example, for the 2000 World March of Women, organizers put in place clear strategies to ensure diversity of representation, specifically from women in the Global South.[11] Intersectionality has also been used as a strategy to confront persistent patterns of privilege and exclusion in organizations and movement spaces.

Decolonization

If we are serious about dismantling systems and structures of oppression, social innovation must be put in service of decolonization. In our own context of Canada, a settler-nation built on stolen land, we must contend with both historical and ongoing colonial violence against Indigenous Peoples. As Eve Tuck, Unangax̂ scholar of Indigenous methodologies and education, and K. Wayne Yang, scholar of decolonization and community organizing, assert, decolonization is not a metaphor.[12] It is not a platitude or vague statement of affinity – it is a direct and specific call for stolen lands to be returned to Indigenous Peoples.

As the national discourse of reconciliation with Indigenous Peoples has taken hold, there is a risk that these efforts become diluted and depoliticized, as happened with social innovation. As Pam Palmater, Mi'kmaq lawyer, professor and activist, argues: "We are running to do good stuff, but we haven't done the hard stuff." She continues:

> Public officials have adopted our calls for decolonization in their bid to promote more superficial forms of reconciliation like changing the names on buildings, placing our art-work on currency, or wearing clothing with Indigenous cultural designs in Parliament. Meanwhile, the crisis issues facing many Indigenous

peoples that have directly resulted from historic and ongoing colonization remain unaddressed.[13]

Michi Saagiig Nishnaabeg scholar, artist and writer Leanne Betasamosake Simpson introduces us to the idea of "acts of resurgence" as something separate and distinct from acts of protest, actions that exist in and of themselves as a form of resistance and challenge. She is critical of Western-based conceptualizations of social movements or collective action, suggesting dominant social movement theories lack an understanding of Indigenous political culture and theory and don't adequately incorporate the context of colonialism. "When resistance is defined solely as large-scale political mobilizations, we miss much of what has kept our languages, cultures, and systems of governance alive."[14] She articulates a different reference point for social justice, not based on Western, liberal philosophy but on her own Nishnaabeg culture, seeing cultural resurgence and resilience as a key manifestation of social justice. Social justice isn't just about large mobilization in the streets; it's also important to "rebuild our culturally inherent philosophical contexts for governance, education, healthcare, and economy" built on values of antiauthoritarianism, nonhierarchical ways of being and anti-essentialism.[15]

Transformative justice

Intersectionality has brought forth important analytic and practical applications for learning spaces and movement work. With an ARAO and decolonial lens, this analysis is further politicized and brings nuance and action to dismantling structures of oppression, centering justice and addressing the root historical and systemic barriers that have created inequalities. Working toward equity and justice, intersectionality recognizes that individuals have different needs, starting points and challenges and considers the diversity of experiences and identities in relation to gender, race, class, disability, sexuality, age and ethnicity. An equity framework also centers on what feminist writer and scholar Sarah Ahmed refers to as "structurally transformative inclusion" and ensures that equity-seeking groups are included in decision-making processes and involved in leading and co-constructing solutions to a more just and equitable society.[16]

Feminism, antiracism and intersectionality discourses have informed critiques of power and privilege and have entered the mainstream. "Call outs" and "cancel culture" involve publicly criticizing individuals or institutional statements, actions and behaviors that are seen as harmful, abusive and/or oppressive. Historically, they have been used as a collective tactic by marginalized groups to question power and challenge corporations, institutions and abusers.[17] Call outs often occur on social media platforms, where they can be shared and spread quickly, and public figures and politicians can be questioned and held accountable for their wrongdoings. In recent years, the far right has weaponized cancel culture, claiming it is a form of harassment and silencing tactic that censors free speech.

As cancel culture has entered the mainstream, this tactic has been misapplied to social movement and community organizing spaces, causing harm and fractures and destabilizing collective power – and also losing the original intent of the tactic to hold powerful public figures accountable. Those involved in social movements need to be held accountable for their actions, and activists need productive ways to call out oppression and deal with conflict. Increasingly, activists, particularly those from traditionally marginalized groups such as Black, Indigenous and People of Color and queer communities are questioning how to hold each other accountable while doing difficult and sometimes even risky social justice work and activism.

Writer, facilitator and activist adrienne maree brown explores the impacts of cancel culture and transformative justice in her work *We Will Not Cancel Us and Other Dreams of Transformative Justice*.[18] While brown recognizes that there is a place and time for "calling out" injustices and holding those who have caused harm (including institutions and organizations) accountable, especially for Black and Brown marginalized communities, she also questions the potential harms and limitations of cancel culture, arguing that the focus on punishment (canceling) can actually limit the potential for individuals to grow and learn from mistakes and thus engage in true accountability and repair. Intersectionality plays an important role here as differing identities and power dynamics will impact experiences of both harm and accountability. Instead, brown advocates for compassion and nuanced reflections that recognize the broader social and systemic context in which harm occurs and foster learning, growth and connection. Navigating conflict and harm in a way that promotes justice, healing and individual and collective transformation builds more resilient communities engaged in social justice. As brown notes:

> We won't end the systemic patterns of harm by isolating and picking off individuals, just as we can't limit the communicative power of mycelium by plucking a single mushroom from the dirt. We need to flood the entire system with life-affirming principles and practices, to clear the channels between us of the toxicity of supremacy, to heal from the harms of a legacy of devaluing some lives and needs in order to indulge others.[19]

If we are truly in movement work for the long haul, we need to make space to hold difficult conversations, to encourage reflexivity in ourselves and others and to address behavior that is harmful and/or abusive in a way that ignites transformative justice practices that center equity, respect and care for one another. Strengthening our movements and goals of transformation with critical thinking skills and powerful applications of feminist intersectionality, decolonization and antiracism fortifies our collective power to create the change we want to see in the world.

6

Acting collectively

Reasons for collective action

The liberatory model of social innovation is based primarily on collective action and social movements. But what exactly does collective action imply? And what is the point of mobilizations that consist, for the most part, of protesting, demonstrating and demanding instead of directly building concrete initiatives to meet the challenges of the present?

Let's start by clarifying the components of collective action. First of all, an action resulting from combined, uncoordinated individual behavior (a traffic jam, for example) cannot be characterized as collective action. The same is true of the impact of fashion, ads that go viral and other social phenomena of imitation, which spread exponentially, without the people involved being conscious of acting with a common goal. In short, collective action is not primarily based on the number of people involved but on the coordination of action to pursue a common goal. Social movements are distinguished from other forms of collective action or participation "by the more assertive protest relationship they have with dominant institutions, which is apparent both in their mobilization dynamics and in the goals of their actions."[1]

This assertive aspect can take the form of a demand for an increased minimum wage, housing rights advocacy, denunciation of sexual violence or opposition to the construction of a pipeline or airport, for example. As we will see later, many major social changes and advances in social justice were achieved through mass mobilizations for equality. These were not the work of a day but the cumulative effect of numerous social struggles that brought about legal, institutional, cultural and structural changes that are simply taken for granted today.

While many social movements aim to embody ideal and new ways of living, other movements fiercely resist specific changes or even campaign against some rights, such as the right to abortion, gender-affirming care for trans people or migrant rights. Social movements are not necessarily progressive, so a critical analysis inspired by a genuine concern for social justice is always the essential starting point.

While social movements can certainly mobilize *for* something (justice, dignity, adoption of a law), mobilizing *against* an adversary, whether the state, a social group, a corporation or another specific form of authority, is invariably an irreducible part of the conflict. Social movements take shape in specific political contexts, and, while they represent a form of political participation, they generally mobilize outside formal institutions and often bring a broad diversity of actors, resources and modes of action into play. We will subsequently see how numerous social innovations emerge from these spaces of collective experiment.

At this point, we could ask what motivates people to mobilize, to invest time and energy in such conflictual arenas. The paradox raised by the economist Mancur Olson shows that while a group of people may have a shared interest to act together for a cause that will benefit them, very often, people do not mobilize.[2] In fact, each person can decide to let others act for them, thus playing the role of a "free rider" who benefits from others' actions without assuming any personal costs. This passive attitude, perfectly logical from an economic rationality perspective, can be seen, for example, during strikes, where a majority often votes in favor of this pressure tactic but only a minority actually joins the picket line. In short, collective action is not a given.

To understand how social movements form despite a rational calculation that might suggest otherwise, we can analyze their various dimensions: triggers, strategies to mobilize resources, the role of the political context and collective identities and so on.

First, among the main engines of mobilization, we find aspirations or desires frustrated by a situation or social order that seems unjust. Discontent, dissatisfaction, anger and moral outrage are important effective levers of collective protest action. In other words, people don't mobilize when things are going well but when many are experiencing a problem or feeling a sense of want, injustice or deprivation.

In response to the question "Why do people rebel?," political scientist Ted Gurr uses the notion of "relative frustration" to describe the potentially explosive gap between the value that a person has at a given moment (whether wealth, status or social recognition) and what they consider to be their right.[3] In other words, people don't mobilize simply because they are poor but because they believe they deserve a better situation which is refused to them.

This, of course, involves a work of interpretation, which gives meaning to one's situation. Collective mobilization is not the mechanical result of something lacking or an irrational frustration but a response to social injustice interpreted as such. As sociologist Erik Neveu states: "A social movement requires a work of producing discourse, an allocation of responsibility, an injection of meaning in experienced social relations."[4]

Through a few historical examples, we can see why long-oppressed people came to gain consciousness of their situation and to act collectively to change the order of things. However, social movements do not emerge spontaneously just because people believe they are experiencing injustice. Very often, collective action remains isolated and leaves no trace, as can be seen with many online petitions or some one-off protests. Thus, the question is not only *why*, in general, collective action arises but *how* a social movement emerges, is organized and fails or succeeds in reaching its objectives.

The art of mobilizing

While we now often contrast the spontaneity of popular mobilizations to the workings of big organizations, such as political parties and unions, social movements owe their effectiveness to an entire labor of organization and mobilization of activist, logistical and financial resources. For a social movement to succeed in making itself felt, a large number of people must be involved, from active members to individuals who support the cause more passively – sympathizers, allies, networks and organizations.

Sociologist Anthony Oberschall's work shows the necessity of mobilizing networks of solidarity and collaboration to give the social movement energy and make it last.[5] If the social groups involved are poorly organized, mobilizations tend to be brief and violent, such as the peasant revolts in Europe from the 14th to 16th centuries or the Paris suburb riots in 2005. The power of the group is not primarily based on the justice of its cause but on its capacity to mobilize diverse resources, as the US civil rights movement shows.[6]

There are multiple social conditions for mobilization. Collective action does not arise in a vacuum but out of background conditions: for example, the strength of social ties, cultural representations or established knowledge of different ways of acting together. Sociologist and political scientist Charles Tilly developed the notion of a "repertoire of collective action" to describe the set of preexisting forms allowing groups to structure their action while leaving room for improvisation according to the context. "Real people do not get together and Act Collectively. They meet to petition Parliament, organize telephone campaigns, demonstrate outside of city hall, attack power looms, go on strike."[7]

These different ways of coming together to protest, make one's voice heard and put pressure on an adversary are not new. Before the Industrial Revolution, most collective action was limited to the local level, whether through diverting popular rituals (such as parodies and carnivals as spaces for social subversion) or patronage (financial or material support from local elites). In the 19th century, we witnessed the gradual emergence of national mobilizations, such as large protests and strikes by the workers' movement and demands directed toward central governments, such as a law to restrict the number of hours in the workday. For a glimpse of the evolution of the repertoire of collective action and the inventiveness of social movements, we can look more closely at the tactical and strategic innovations of the different movements marking the 20th century.

The civil rights movement in the US was particularly creative in its mobilization techniques. The Montgomery bus boycott campaign, for example, was organized to oppose racial segregation in public transport. After Rosa Parks was arrested and sentenced for public disorder in 1955 for refusing to give up her seat to a White passenger on a bus, activists gathered at the Baptist Church on Dexter Avenue and founded the Montgomery Improvement Association, of which Martin Luther King was to become president. While the Black community had already been mobilized for some time, a new tactic emerged. Precise demands were formulated, 35,000 flyers were distributed and the idea of nonviolent civil disobedience was embodied in concrete action: refuse to take the bus until racial segregation in public transport ended. After 381 days of boycott, on 13 November 1956, the Supreme Court of the United States declared that segregation on buses was unconstitutional.

Another innovation of the civil rights movement was the sit-in, which first appeared on 4 February 1960 in a North Carolina grocery store. Instead of the usual large marches, the sit-in consisted of remaining in a seated position for as long as possible in a public street or a private or public establishment to deliberately obstruct a busy area and draw attention to an overlooked social problem. This tactic of disobedience triggered strong reactions from store owners, White people and officials, who increased their violent attacks on the protestors. However, since the sit-in was easy to film and photograph, this form of collective action had a strong impact on public opinion. Many variants of the sit-in followed – teach-in, pray-in, swim-in, read-in – to occupy places formerly reserved for White people: universities, churches, pools, libraries and so on. These diverse tactics were quickly picked up by other social movements, thus broadening their own repertoires of collective action.

The women's movement has also used a multitude of techniques to make their voices heard across history. A wide assortment of tactics has been mobilized, including the petitions, marches and direct action of the movement for the right to vote in different countries in the 19th century; feminist self-awareness groups; and the social media campaign of the #MeToo movement to denounce sexual assault and harassment.

At the beginning of the century, suffragettes organized large and colorful parades, but they also used other more or less radical forms of action. For example, in 1905, two activists, Christabel Pankhurst and Annie Kenney, disrupted a meeting of the (British) Liberal Party by shouting slogans; they also chose to go to prison rather than pay a fine to raise public sympathy. Some incarcerated suffragettes opted for a hunger strike as a protest, while others set fire to a theater, sent parcel bombs with phosphorus flakes and carried out bomb attacks on places symbolizing male supremacy.

In the 1970s, new demands around sexuality, family, work, the right to abortion and conjugal violence emerged.[8] Feminists organized shelters for survivors of sexual assault and domestic violence, self-managed daycares and engaged in other organizational forms promoting women's liberation.

In the 1980s, various feminist trends introduced new frameworks of analysis and methods of mobilization rooted in different collective identities. The contributions of Black, Chicana, Indigenous, lesbian and trans feminists complicated the understanding of gender relations relative to other social relations, which had an impact on organizational dynamics (the critique of racism and "White feminism" within feminist movements is a good example).

In the 1990s, the feminist movement also specifically focused on actions with media reach, including music groups, fanzine production and internet blogs. This method now translates especially into increased use of digital technologies and social media: production of images, videos and educational material on different themes (for example, consent, rape culture, gender identities) and the multiplication of women-only online mutual aid groups.[9] New digital platforms contribute to the rapid spread of testimonies and denunciations using hashtags such as #MeToo, #BalanceTonPorc and #NiUnaMenos, which accelerated the transnational circulation of feminist discourses and demands.

The circulation of tactics is not limited to a single movement but allows cross-fertilization among a multitude of mobilizations and social movements. For example, the tactic of identify-specific spaces coming out of feminism has been adopted by queer, antiracist and Indigenous movements, who transform it in their own way. The circulation of tactics is thus not the simple dissemination of activist practices but a real source of innovation.

Between social movements and innovations

The social movements described in this chapter are primarily based on a strong mobilization of affected individuals and social groups, which distinguish them from traditional structures, such as political parties, unions, nongovernmental organizations and environmental organizations, which, despite a very large number of members, are mainly led by professionals seeking to influence elites and public policies. Social movements are also different from community service organizations and self-organized solidarity networks, which primarily aim to meet the needs of their members.

Many social innovations emerge from service organizations and mutual aid groups, including community organizations, community economic development corporations and social economy enterprises. The idea is to invent new ways of producing, housing, feeding and meeting the needs of the community rather than campaigning for rights and obtaining gains from the state. In this way, we could say that social innovations are primarily geared toward the creation of new solutions to specific social challenges, while social movements remain focused on challenging the establishment.

However, it would be a mistake to make too sharp a distinction between these different types of social organizations, which, in practice, collaborate and influence each other. The same actors often circulate from one organization to the other. For example, it is not uncommon to see a student movement activist become a community or union organizer and then a candidate for a political party. Community organizations and coalitions fighting for human rights are often an integral part of larger social movements. Moreover, strikes and strong popular mobilizations foster the emergence of social innovations, which continue to exist after the movement has fizzled out.

To give just one example, the Idle No More movement, founded in December 2012 in reaction to the Canadian government's C-45 omnibus bill, which made it possible to violate ancestral treaties, was one of the largest Indigenous mobilizations in recent decades in Canada. Following a call-out by four women, tens of thousands of Indigenous people from all across Canada mobilized by organizing flash mobs in shopping malls, traditional dances in public spaces, blockades of pipelines, roads and highways as well as various speaking occasions inspired by the principle of nonviolent civil disobedience.

In addition to these diverse forms of protest, which generated unprecedented attention to Indigenous issues in the public sphere, including the official recognition of cultural genocide and missing and murdered Indigenous women and girls, other initiatives were launched. In Canada, the self-financed One House Many Nations campaign, launched in October 2015, collected funds to build ecological and affordable tiny homes for Indigenous people and homeless people.[10] The shift from protest to social innovation was undertaken out of respect for the values of dignity, mutual aid, human rights and social and environmental justice. In this case, social innovation was not born out of a nice idea by benevolent young entrepreneurs but the result of a social mobilization aiming to transform the conditions of the existence of oppressed peoples. While social innovation does not always come out of social movements, collective action very often acts as a catalyst for new ideas and inspiring projects.

In sum, social movements help to change society in three main ways. First, social mobilizations often bring about innovations in tactics and strategies and thus enlarge the repertoire of collective action. For example, the "plaza" movement (Mothers of the Plaza de Mayo in Argentina, 15-M in Spain, Occupy Wall Street in the United States and Nuit debout in France) helped make the occupation of public squares into a crucible for renewing practices of direct democracy, consensus decision making and other self-organization techniques. These movements also saw the emergence of mutual aid groups, solidarity cooperatives and other innovative collective projects in big-city neighborhoods.

Second, social movements are also incubators, even accelerators, of liberatory social innovation. Collective action represents an excellent means of raising awareness and mobilizing the community, which then becomes more receptive to new solutions. In addition, mobilization helps develop organizational capacity, the power to act and a feeling of control over reality. The word empowerment can be used to describe this process of collective learning, which is stimulated by the self-organization of those affected.

Sociologist Zeynep Tufekci, in responding to the often-asked question "Do protests even work?," shares that "yes, of course protests work, but usually not in the way and timeframe that many people think. Protests sometimes look like failures in the short term, but much of the power of protests is in their long-term effects, on both the protesters themselves and the rest of society."[11]

Finally, through repeated collective action and perseverance, social movements contribute to large-scale social change. Historically marginalized and oppressed groups such as women, racialized and nonbinary people wouldn't have the same rights today if it weren't for the many social struggles waged by their members, sometimes at the cost of their health or even their lives. While these rights are too often still under threat, the combination of direct action and advocacy, claims making and a good deal of determination have nevertheless brought institutional changes and improved the conditions of life for people from marginalized, excluded and oppressed groups. For instance, in the face of anti-trans rhetoric and actions in North America, we've seen impressive counter-protests affirming the rights of the trans community.

None of this was achieved overnight. Each time, pressure was necessary to change public opinion and the position of government officials. What kinds of approaches can be used to achieve this? Diverse strategies can help to express ideas that may begin as minority positions but can come to form the shared meaning of the next era.

7

Driving change

Symbolic construction of the social

Successful social change involves the transition between local and specific innovations, such as the tactical innovations discussed in the previous chapter and broader macrosocial, structural transformations. If social movements are to transform social relations, it is not enough that they simply know how to mobilize resources or choose the right tactic from their repertoire of collective action. As this chapter will highlight, their actions must also *make sense* to the actors involved. An entire labor of interpretation must go into ensuring that the people affected perceive their condition as unjust or intolerable and are motivated to act to change things. We must be able to name, *blame* and *claim* to orient our collective action.[1]

Naming allows a situation to be defined as problematic or unjust, whether for a specific group or the population in general. Blaming allows for the attribution of fault to a person, group, institution or social structure, that is, to attribute the situation to causes, individuals or institutions. Finally, claiming formulates a response to the problem: demands or actions are defined to transform the state of things. These three functions are essential to the symbolic construction of social movements, which must expose as unacceptable a situation previously presented as normal, natural or inevitable.

This is not a simple matter of promoting an ideology or constructing reality to serve one's interests in a conflict. The "putting into protest language" always involves a *cognitive* dimension, gathering facts and data to understand a social phenomenon deserving our attention. But this construction of meaning goes beyond the descriptive: it is *critical* and *normative*, foregrounding hidden relations of domination and a moral evaluation of a situation considered harmful, unjust or immoral. Finally, the symbolic construction of social movements involves an *identity* dimension, within which a group of people with a shared reality ("us") and an enemy ("them") is defined.

The construction of identity in social movements almost always goes both ways. As sociologist Erik Neveu notes: "Identity is the result of the unceasing labor of negotiation between acts of *attribution*, principles of identification coming from the other, and actions of *belonging* aimed at expressing one's identity, categories in which the individual intends to be perceived."[2] To take the example of people who carry out direct actions during protests: in activist circles, they define themselves as black bloc, but they are often perceived in mainstream media and public opinion as "hooligans." And while, these days, self-identification is given importance, individual and collective identity still inevitably arise from interactions between an individual and their environment, group and society. The entire strategic work of social movements is to redefine the dynamics of situations, affected individuals and those held responsible in order to rectify a situation perceived as unacceptable.

Collective identities are complex. In addition to religious and ethnic diversity, contemporary societies are marked by multiple forms of identity defined by social relations of class and gender, sexual orientation, nationality, ability and more. In this context, it is ever more difficult to have recourse to general categories such as working class, nation or even women in a generic sense, as certain forms of exclusion can be produced even within these groups.

In reality, each one of us bears multiple identities. An individual can simultaneously be a woman, mother, employee, Black, heterosexual, in good physical condition and privileged in some contexts and facing discrimination in others. Activism and social organizations can no longer abstract from the personal experience of affected individuals and the complex power relations that shape their reality.

Moreover, one must remember that identity is not an immutable essence but a relationship and a social construct. The production of meaning is, therefore, an irreducible dimension of social movements: they must continuously strive to modify collective representations to assert discontent, denounce a shared problem or expose other forms of social suffering. The objective is always to challenge problematic social situations that can be transformed. To do this, we must construct shared significations capable of motivating us to action.

A matter of framing

A useful term to analyze the construction of meaning by social movements is "framing." The concept of the "frame" was developed by sociologist Erving Goffman to describe interpretative schema allowing individuals to orient themselves in the world.[3] At the collective level, we can talk about the meanings that help groups take action and obtain public legitimacy. These representations are too often conceived as static, frozen beliefs passively adopted by individuals. The verb "frame" highlights the active *process* of agents deliberately constructing their discourse in a specific context to maximize their impact on society. To mobilize effectively, one must know how to frame.

Sociologists and social movement scholars Robert D. Benford and David A. Snow distinguish three essential framing operations: *diagnostic* framing (name, blame); *prognostic* framing (claim); and *motivational* framing (invoking, for example, the gravity or urgency of the situation to motivate people to act).[4] There is also an entire series of more specific framings, such as the framing of borders and adversaries (between *us* and *them*), and counterframing, which attempts to circumvent labels imposed by movement adversaries. For example, the 2012 student strike in Quebec was quickly characterized as a "boycott" by the government, while protestors were often called "hooligans" and radical activists "terrorists."

Frames can be more or less flexible or rigid, inclusive or exclusive. Some confine themselves to the interests of a specific group, while others attempt to expand the mobilization beyond those primarily concerned, as in the slogan, "La grève est étudiante, la lutte est populaire" (Student strike, people's struggle).

It is possible to frame a discourse to enlarge its significance, but the social, cultural and political context in which it will disseminate must be taken into account. In other words, framing requires an ability to *read* the social context so that demands are not only heard but perceived as credible and convincing. The goal of the process of framing is thus to produce a message that *resonates* with the target audience.

The resonance of a frame depends on several factors, including its *credibility* and its *relative pertinence* to those targeted by the mobilization. The credibility of a discourse relies on its coherence, its plausibility and the credibility of the actors propagating it.[5] Pertinence refers to its capacity to capture the attention of certain people. A frame can be pertinent because it speaks to people's values or profound convictions, because it connects to lived experiences or because it resonates with the stories, myths or other narratives of a given culture.

Affects, the social imaginary and shared meaning have a direct effect on the resonance of collective action. Framing, often underestimated by people who want to change the world, is key to the success of social movements. Actors must explain why and how we can change a situation and why we must act now.

To avoid reinventing the wheel, we can draw on a repertoire of "master frames" that seem to recur in various mobilizations. As Benford and Snow emphasize:

> Only a handful of collective action frames have been identified as being sufficiently broad in interpretive scope, inclusivity, flexibility, and cultural resonance to function as master frames, including rights frames (Valocchi 1996, Williams & Williams 1995), choice frames (Davies 1999), injustice frames (Carroll & Ratner 1996a,b, Gamson et al 1982), environmental justice frames (Cable & Shriver 1995, Čapek 1993), culturally pluralist frames (Berbier 1998, Davies 1999), sexual terrorism frames (Jenness & Broad 1994), oppositional frames (Blum-Kulka & Liebes 1993, Coy & Woehrle 1996), hegemonic frames (Blum-Kulka & Liebes 1993), and a "return to Democracy" frame (Noonan 1995).[6]

Public relations: the tools of framing

How can we affect how an issue is framed in the public space? Social movements and community initiatives face two significant problems when interacting with the public sphere. First, they don't have many resources to reach their goals and accomplish their core activities; therefore, they often consider that using these resources in public relations or communication cannot be their priority. Second, they usually have opponents – big corporations, governments and elite groups – who have the money, the expertise and the staff to interact efficiently with media and journalists. Many movements face the same question: How do we influence the framing of the issues that matter to us with modest means and powerful opponents?

From the 1970s to the end of the 1990s, various scholars made a powerful critique of the public relations industry's disastrous impact on citizens' capacity to voice their concerns about an issue and change a situation they considered unjust.[7] These critiques not only led to a better understanding of the strategies of the powerful when it came to defending their interest but also produced the idea of using the tools of public relations, giving it an activist twist. Organizations like Greenpeace and Sea Shepherd were some of the earliest adopters of these strategies, organizing large-scale symbolic gestures that would attract cameras worldwide. The idea of Guerilla PR was quickly popularized in the 1990s and 2000s through actions like those of the Yes Men,[8] a group of activists who showed the hypocrisy of big corporations and government by enacting false media events that received very real attention.

Nowadays, basic public relations are not that complicated and can be done on a very low budget. What one mainly needs is time. Building a list of media contacts interested in your issue should be the priority, and with a bit of time, you'll see this list grow to a very decent size. The second priority should be the creation of a space where you can provide text, press releases, photos and videos about what your group does. Whether this is a complete website or a simple social media account, it doesn't matter: as long as you let people know that it is there, they can get information from you. The last priority is to establish a network of allies to coordinate with. When you bring more people in, it's important to develop a plan of how to interact with the media so you avoid stepping on anyone's toes.

In terms of skills, the most important ones to develop can be learned by anyone. Knowing how to write a press release – for example, not telling a story in chronological order but starting with the most important news in the lead – is useful. Two or three hours with someone who knows how to do this will be enough to learn the tricks; the rest will come with practice. A second skill is the art of giving interviews. Training a few spokespersons can be done pretty quickly by doing fake interviews, filming them and practicing to better the results, but again, only practice in a real studio setting will make perfect. Learning how to organize media events, such as press conferences, briefings and scrums, is also helpful. Knowing how and when to invite journalists to an event, where to locate them and at what time of day is nothing tricky, but it gives better results.

So, there is no need to choose between action and framing. Most organizations and movements can do both. Public relations is not something that only professionals can do. Activists can learn, practice guerrilla-style and get good results. Regardless of the skill set, the results will always be better than leaving the media alone to understand your action or, even worse, letting your opponent do the public relations work.

Social movements and discursive strategies

The best way to understand a process of framing is to analyze a concrete historical example. Framing is not only used by social movements but by any form of organization that attempts to influence public opinion and legitimize its actions by means of advertising, public relations campaigns or marketing, for example. In Canada, the mobilization to save the Montfort Hospital, threatened with closure after budget cuts by the Ontario government in 1996, provides an example.

When Conservative premier Mike Harris was elected in Ontario in 1995, he planned to introduce austerity measures by framing his program around the idea of a "common sense revolution." The CAD$150 million projected cut in the Ottawa region involved closing the Montfort Hospital, a real symbol for the Franco-Ontarian community, who were particularly affected by the austerity measures.

A strong mobilization followed the announcement, and the SOS Montfort coalition relied on a motivational framing emphasizing the urgency of acting to stop the government's decision. What might have appeared as an isolated case or collateral effect of more general cuts was soon framed as a matter of linguistic rights and a national issue extending far beyond the interests of Franco-Ontarians in the Ottawa region. The movement rapidly won the support of politicians, notably from Quebec. In March 1997, Quebec premier Lucien Bouchard spoke out about it: "It's a fundamental question of language rights, it is inconceivable that this hospital should close."[9]

The master framing of the defense of rights thus served as the movement's spearhead, combined with the principle of respect for linguistic rights, since Montfort Hospital as an institution was considered a key safeguard for the Franco-Ontarian community:

> On 29 November 1999, the Divisional Court of Ontario ruled in favor of SOS Montfort activists … In their decision, they clarified that "What is at stake in these proceedings is not simply a minority language issue or a minority education issue. What is at stake is a minority culture issue." In other words, institutions are essential to the survival of cultural communities.[10]

Idle No More is another example.[11] In terms of framing, the ideas of dignity, autonomy and collective assertion are expressed in the very name of the movement.

Another form of framing, reflected in recourse to the expression "cultural genocide," stirred up controversy after it received widespread public attention in the wake of the publication of Canada's 2015 Truth and Reconciliation Report.[12] Far from being anodyne, this formulation called attention to the process of assimilation and erasure of Indigenous cultures and Peoples, among other things, through residential schools. This framing exposed the seriousness of the problem and attributed serious fault to the Canadian state, guilty of having closed its eyes to this phenomenon for too long (diagnostic framing). The naming and blaming, and then demanding of recognition, spotlighted a phenomenon long considered marginal or inconsequential.

It is interesting to note that the framing strategies used by social movements are often employed by actors and organizations trying to convey their demands in the political arena: for example, new political figures and formations such as Podemos (Spain), La France insoumise, Bernie Sanders (United States) and Québec solidaire all resort to "left populism" to reframe political issues.

While right populism aims to accentuate and widen the gap between the people and the elite, between ordinary people and the oligarchy, conservative populism tends to define the people according to a majority cultural identity to the exclusion of minorities. Left populism, on the other hand, deploys a framing of adversaries by defining the people in a democratic and pluralist way. This discourse is addressed to people as *citizens* and *active participants* in a political community and not as individual bearers of homogenous cultural values (an ethnic *us*) or with rights as consumers or contributors.

The left-populist strategy thus aims to construct a *popular subject* beyond leftist activists and people who are already on side, bringing together a *political majority* capable of adhering to a broad democratic project of social transformation. As the division between left and right now seems blurred in a context marked by the rise of populist, conservative and extreme right forces, the framing strategy is to resignify notions such as people, nation, country, democracy, equality and popular sovereignty to prevent parties opposed to social change and minority rights from imposing their vision of the world on large swathes of the population. Left populism aims in this way to increase its cultural resonance through an inclusive redefinition of the people and the narrative of a "return to democracy" as a counterweight to the frame illustrated by the slogan "Make America Great Again."

Sometimes the discursive framing itself becomes a point of contestation, as we saw with the Black Lives Matter movement and attempts by detractors to advance Blue Lives Matter and All Lives Matter framings to discredit them. Struggles over access to reproductive justice have also been the site of fierce battles over framing – pro-life versus pro-choice, anti-choice versus pro-abortion. The fact that so much energy is spent debating framings highlights the importance of discursive power in social transformation.

Of course, we cannot change the world through rhetorical strategies nor through the impact of discourse in the arena of social movements, public space and the parliamentary sphere alone. Social transformation involves profound changes within the different economic, political and cultural layers of society. Nevertheless, the strategic importance of framing, the symbolic construction of collective action and the central role of meaning must never be underestimated. They can have an enormous impact on mobilizations. Some movements have a huge resonance with the population, while others never extend beyond a handful of people who are already on board. The reach of a movement is no mystery, however, as many historical examples demonstrate. The latter can teach us about the best ways to drive social change through the art of discourse.

8

Transforming the economy

A brief definition of capitalism

When we begin to look at the best ways of transforming the economic system, we must understand exactly what we're talking about. The first thing we think about when we hear the word "economy" is the "production" or "market" economy. This is based on the production of goods by wage labor, generating a profit for owners or shareholders of the company – whether a small or medium enterprise, an oil company, a service station, a multinational firm, a shopping center, a chain of restaurants, a real estate company, a private bank, a media conglomerate or a digital platform such as Uber, Facebook and Google.

Here we must distinguish small property – house, car or computer, for example – from private ownership of the *means of production*, which engenders structural inequality between two social classes. On the one hand, there are those who control the vast majority of economic resources and investment capacity and can thereby enrich themselves through the accumulation of industrial, commercial and financial capital. On the other hand, there are those who are forced to work to earn an income and meet their basic needs. Of course, the entire picture is more complex because there are working middle and upper classes, each with their own differences and contradictions. It is nevertheless the case that the capitalist system tends to encourage the concentration of wealth in the hands of a few through a process of capital accumulation that never ceases to increase social inequalities, as we showed in Chapter 1.

In sum, capitalism can be defined as a complex process of production and circulation in which the production, exchange and consumption of commodities are tools for the accumulation of wealth. This dynamic of value accumulation is not a result of the individual will of "wealthy entrepreneurs" or "capitalists" but is a product of the system itself, which pushes everyone, from the poorest to the wealthiest, to participate in this logic.[1] This translates into an irresistible drive toward economic growth, technological innovation, geographic expansion, colonization of new spheres of activity and social acceleration.[2] In addition to exacerbating economic inequalities, capitalism relies on various mechanisms such as exploitation, expropriation, alienation and erosion.

Exploitation refers to the process by which a minority appropriates wealth produced by "free" wage labor. *Expropriation*, or "accumulation by dispossession," describes the appropriation of wealth or resources through coercion, theft or force: seizing lands, colonization, privatization of public services, patents on seeds and so on. *Alienation* designates the feeling of being cut off from the fruits of one's labor, from others and from the world; to no longer be in a relationship with one's environment; to no longer be in control of one's own activity or existence. Finally, *erosion* refers to the way the economic system puts excessive pressure on the free resources and institutions that enable social life: destruction of ecosystems, loss of legitimacy of democratic institutions, growing exhaustion of health and education staff, increase of burnouts and so on.

Political philosopher Nancy Fraser thus argues that capitalism should not only be seen as an *economic system* based on private property, wage labor, accumulation and the preponderant role of the market in the allocation of resources but also as an *institutionalized social order*.[3] She is referring to the fact that the capitalist society is constituted by structural divisions between the economy and nature, the economic and the political, the economy and social reproduction (that is, all of the activities that regenerate social relations and the labor force). Commodity production is dependent on background conditions, such as the preservation of ecosystems, the state maintaining a certain social stability and all the invisible gendered labor of care in the domestic and community sectors.[4] According to Fraser, the process of capitalist accumulation destabilizes its own conditions of possibility, thus introducing a *tendency toward crisis* in different spheres:

> In the case of its ecological conditions, what is at risk are the natural processes that sustain life … In the case of its social-reproduction conditions, what is imperilled are the sociocultural processes that supply the solidary relations, affective dispositions and value horizons that underpin social cooperation, while also furnishing the appropriately socialized and skilled human beings who constitute "labour". In the case of its political conditions, what is compromised are the public powers, both national and transnational, that guarantee property rights, enforce contracts, adjudicate disputes, quell anti-capitalist rebellions and maintain the money supply.[5]

This brief portrait of capitalism may appear both totalizing and paralyzing, as though we were all imprisoned in an iron cage with no room for maneuver. Fortunately, capitalism is not a totalitarian system but an unstable social formation with numerous contradictions. Commodity production continues to rely on noncommodified social spheres, and there are multiple forms of economic activity that escape the logic of profit maximization.

Different spheres of the economy

While the capitalist market economy is currently the predominant mode of production of goods and services, plenty of other ways of organizing the satisfaction of human needs exist alongside it: nonprofit social enterprises, local systems of exchange, informal mutual aid networks, solidarity cooperatives, state corporations, to name but a few. The expression "plural economy" is used precisely to highlight this diversity of economic forms (beyond the private sector), which is becoming the norm within our collective imaginary. A more global picture can be obtained by analyzing the various spheres of material and economic life in turn.

In the first place, the market economy is defined in relation to another economy, in a dynamic of coexistence, collaboration and opposition: the so-called "public" or "planned" economy, which we can characterize more precisely as a "state" economy. The so-called private economy, in fact, also acts in the public sphere broadly understood (as opposed to the intimate sphere of friend and family relations), and capitalist corporations, just as hierarchical and centralized as state institutions, use economic planning on a scale that can greatly surpass some states. To simplify our analysis, we will nevertheless adopt the common notions that distinguish market and state, private and public economies.

The state economy is established by civil servants using resources levied by taxes, and it is led by the impact of public debate, social mobilizations and internal struggles within the government and civil service to determine the allocation of resources according to the (perceived) needs of the population. We can immediately think of jobs in public administration, public services, education and health and social services, as well as state-owned companies and publicly funded institutions.

The overall picture also includes the social and solidarity economy, encompassing the entire range of economic activities carried out by collective enterprises (nonprofits, mutuals, cooperatives) that work in numerous areas: environment, culture, neighborhood services, education, childcare and so on. Sometimes dubbed the "civil society," "third sector" or "nonprofit sector," which takes care of matters neglected by state and market, the social economy can be distinguished from cultural and sporting associations, private clubs, churches, nongovernmental organizations (NGOs) and community organizations by the fact that it produces goods and services sold on the market. It also includes for-profit cooperatives such as farming co-ops and credit unions.

A fourth sphere, often neglected, appears here: social reproductive labor, mostly unpaid, invisibilized and mainly done by women, and in particular racialized women in the context of paid work.[6] The gendered division between public and private, market production and reproduction of the labor force conceals a vast amount of material, relational and symbolic labor, from household chores to other activities essential to social life. This includes "healthcare, development and transformation of knowledge, values and cultural practices, as well as the construction of individual and collective identities."[7] The tripartition of market economy, public economy and social economy thus obscures an entire aspect of economic reality that underlies the "formal economy" of paid jobs.

Social reproduction activities are sometimes paid: for example, in social economy enterprises (such as public daycare centers) or public health and education systems, where women often form the majority of the labor force. Social reproduction can also be undertaken by for-profit enterprises, such as private daycares and clinics, providing income to precarious workers such as cleaning women, who are often from disadvantaged and racialized groups. Nevertheless, the vast majority of social reproduction activities, including education and childcare, household chores and caregiving, remain invisible and undervalued; this labor is rarely included in economic statistics.

Additionally, we can also observe community and self-production economic activities based on principles of giving, mutual aid and reciprocity. While the *social economy* refers to the market activities of associations and cooperatives, this *solidarity economy* embraces a broader sphere of activities, often falling into the vague category of the informal economy.[8] This is the space where people carry out projects together outside the logic of accumulation. Philosopher André Gorz uses "self-production" or "work for oneself" to describe activities as diverse as knitting and gardening, personal or collective artistic projects, community activities such as spaghetti dinners, barter and exchange of services among neighbors and all other activity organized in networks larger than the family and loved ones.[9]

As we can see, the plural economy thus includes a broad range of activities of production, exchange and consumption, allowing diverse needs to be met. Moreover, it is imperative to look beyond the tripartite private/public/collective, which tends to suppress social reproduction and self-production labor as well as informal exchange. That said, it would be naïve to celebrate the plural economy in its current form while capitalism not only continues to dominate the formal economy but often defines our relationship to the world through its ideological pressure and alienation. To expand the place of the public, social, domestic and solidarity economy in our lives, we must figure out ways of multiplying the spaces in which a postcapitalist economy can develop.

Moving beyond the capitalist economy

A first strategy to help build a postcapitalist economy is creating spaces outside the traditional forms of the market economy. By adopting a typology developed by geographers J.K. Gibson-Graham (see Table 8.1), we can identify an entire spectrum of transactions, categories of labor and enterprises that can be more, or less, capitalist.

The general strategy is to reduce the place of the private sector, market transactions and capitalist enterprises in the economy to encourage the spread of alternative, noncapitalist models. Erik Olin Wright's strategy of real utopias seeks to multiply concrete

Table 8.1: Typography of capitalist labor and enterprise

Transactions	Labor	Enterprise
Market	Wage	Capitalist
• Goods and services provided in supermarkets • Real estate market • Bank loans • Financial investments	• Private sector employee • Civil servant • Teacher • Nursing staff • NGO employee	• Retail store • Private bank • Internet giant • Restaurant chain • Private clinic
Alternative market	Alternative paid work	Alternative business
• Local trading systems • Complementary money • Public market • Barter • Fair trade	• Self-employed • Fixed-term contract • Micro-entrepreneur • Independent farming entrepreneur • In-kind payment	• Socially responsible firm • Certified B Corporations* • Social enterprise • State-owned enterprise
Nonmarket	Unpaid	Noncapitalist
• Sharing food • Gift giving • Shared childcare • Gleaning	• Volunteer • Housework • Neighborhood work • Family care • Open-source programming	• Collective enterprise • Cooperative platform • Commons • Self-managed organization • Commune

Note: * Certified B Corporations are corporations certified by the non-profit network B Lab, pertaining to a range of social, environmental and governance standards.

Source: Gibson-Graham, 2006, pp 174–5. Copyright 2006 by the Regents of the University of Minnesota. Reproduced with permission.

alternatives in the interstices of the current system and gradually build a new economic structure through institutional reforms with the potential of supporting postcapitalist social innovations.

This is not about promoting a single sector – public economy or social economy, for example – but about giving greater place to activities that are invisibilized, marginalized or stifled by the dominant model. While there is currently no clear pathway to building a real plural economy, a first step could be to significantly increase resources for the development of noncapitalist initiatives, strengthen support for social innovation projects or multiply solidarity and social economy incubators.

Building a plural economy simultaneously serves several objectives. First, it can help individuals free themselves from dynamics of exploitation and directly influence the organization of their work. A "self-management" perspective, which will be further elaborated in Chapter 10, is all about increasing the democratic power of workers in the production process, with the goal of producing within a nonhierarchical structure. Looking at the largest organizations, it is even possible to imagine the democratization of the governance of companies and public institutions so that a greater number of people come to act directly on the decisions that shape their existence.

Beyond corporate democracy and the democratization of work,[10] this strategy involves broadening participation in community development and finding meaning in one's actions. A plurality of local initiatives, social innovations and alternative economic organizations can help communities meet their needs directly, without waiting for state intervention or private enterprises or placing the responsibility on families. These organizations, rooted in local communities, cannot be relocated for economic reasons because their main objective is not maximizing profit. The goal of the plural economy is to allow people to become participants in the development of their environment, as we will see in Chapter 10.

Toward an entirely democratized economy

We must not underestimate the limits of the social economy, still confined to a marginal share of jobs and gross domestic product

(GDP), around 5 to 10 percent, depending on the country. Many dream of a slow, continuous growth of this economy, but can we imagine that it will ever exceed 20 percent without a deep transformation of economic structures?

One of the problems with the plural economy perspective lies in the (intentional or unintentional) reproduction of a sectorial concept of the economy, which looks to the social economy to fill the gap between the two. How can we hope for a global transformation of the model of development while the dominant economic vision suggests we need to find the right balance between these three pillars?[11] Today it seems necessary to look for a more general frame that entirely rethinks the space occupied by each type of economy, including a reimagining of the boundary between market production and social reproduction.

Moreover, even if we advocate for the multiplication of cooperatives, nonprofit organizations and socially responsible private enterprises, they will continue to develop within the competitive environment of the market economy. In the current circumstances, noncapitalist enterprises remain in the grip of the imperative of competition and are disadvantaged with respect to large companies, which are not tied down by criteria of equity, justice and democracy and can reduce salaries at will or enter merciless commercial wars. Adding to the capitalist system's constraints of accumulation, constant innovation and productivity, this dynamic constitutes a structural impediment to the development of other models. However, the plural economy is incapable of envisaging economic coordination institutions outside the market. On a macroeconomic level, it is plural in name only, leaving the responsibility for resource distribution to the hegemony of the market, a process with foreseeable consequences.

While the idea of planning is now discredited downstream of the excesses of the former Soviet Union's authoritarian regimes, the institution of the market has become *naturalized*, that is, the market appears to be the only possible way to coordinate economic activity. To break free from this sterile dichotomy between market and centralized planning, we need to begin sketching the outline of a global, liberatory project. We must go further and think about the institutional bases of a *democratized, collective economy*, the foundation of a new mode of postcapitalist production.

Some thinkers have tried to take up the challenge by developing a general model starting from lived experiences, analyzing historical examples of movements that attempted economic transformation or thinking speculatively about hypothetical economic structures. Writers such as Murray Bookchin, Michael Albert, Robin Hahnel, Diane Elson, Pat Devine, Paul Cockshott, Allin Cottrell, Marta Harnecker and Erik Olin Wright have constructed theoretical and practical frameworks to facilitate the construction of postcapitalist societies.[12]

When the USSR crumbled in 1991, this debate took a new turn, with two opposing camps: *market socialism* proposed models where worker-led cooperatives competed in a controlled market, while *democratic economic planning* put political mechanisms at the center of the economic process in order to make economic decisions democratically without markets being central to its functioning. Since 2015, the debate about which economic model could replace capitalism has been reenergized by a new dynamism: a vast quantity of books, articles and special issues of scholarly journals have been published, and many conferences and seminars have been organized to further these conversations.

While previous debates centered on the division between markets and plans, current publications take up a wider variety of questions. Two are prominent: first, the development of new technologies and the possibilities and risks they pose for a society free from capitalism, and two, the respect of ecological boundaries while satisfying populations' needs. Other preoccupations also arose including gender and racial relations, global exchanges and conflict management.

While we cannot dive into the pros and cons of each of these economic models here, we can underline the importance of asking what a postcapitalist society could look like. These questions and the resulting discussions feed the flame of hope and create a guiding star to follow in the midst of social transformation.

Although it does not summarize these multiple models, there seems to be a certain convergence around the idea of *economic democracy*, which would include workplace self-management as well as some degree of democratic planning. Many elements must be discussed more broadly, including the role of the market, the place of money, the allocation of surplus as well as the social and ecological criteria to govern production, exchange and the consumption of goods and services. Some models, such as the participatory economy outlined by Albert and Hahnel, represent highly coherent *systems* in which there is no state, no market, no money and are thus pretty distant from the world we live in.

The wealth of the commons

To build an economic democracy based on democratic planning, noncapitalist organizations, the satisfaction of social needs and the respect of planetary limits, a growing number of activists, academics and politicians argue that we must protect and expand the sphere of the "commons." According to philosopher and sociologist Pierre Dardot and Christian Laval:

> The demand for the commons was first brought into existence by social and cultural struggles against the capitalist order and the entrepreneurial state. A central term in the alternative to neoliberalism, the "common" has become the effective principle of the struggles and movements that, over the past two decades, have resisted the dynamics of capital and given rise to original forms of action and discourse.[13]

Indeed, the concept of the commons has become one of the main ideas of antiglobalization, ecology and anticapitalist movements, which are fighting against the current wave of enclosures of land, seeds, ideas and the web. What's more, a whole scientific, academic and activist literature on the commons has been propelled by the work of Nobel Prize-winning economist Elinor Ostrom, following the publication of her book *Governing of the Commons* in 1990.[14] She analyzed common-pool resources, that is, nonexclusive but rival goods such as fishing grounds and irrigation systems, which can be administered equitably, efficiently and sustainably by a community of participants without the need for private or state ownership.

The commons have a very long history and can take many forms depending on local contexts, norms and customs that enable shared resources to be managed collectively over time. This is the first characteristic of the commons, which are "environment-sensitive," meaning that their configuration always depends on the local particularities – ecosystems, communities and territories – in which they take root. Urban and rural commons, public spaces or communal lands, watersheds or housing cooperatives can thus respond to different needs, adapt to several circumstances and be embodied in varied models.

The commons are not based on private property or market logic but on the principles of sharing, access and use. They thus enable us to radically rethink property rights, distinguishing between "inclusive" (access, management, use) and "exclusive" (exclusion, alienation) rights. Whereas private property limits access, management and use of a good or resource to its owner, who can exclude others from using, destroying or reselling it, the commons must be governed through an approach based on participation, collaboration and self-management. For example, a community land trust is a form of collective ownership of land that is entrusted to a not-for-profit organization that must preserve its long-term vocation, whether, for example, for agriculture, conservation of a natural area or affordable housing. The flexible formula of this land common allows a plurality of uses to be accommodated, with some community trusts combining affordable single-family homes, protection of a local forest, community gardens and urban farms.[15]

The commons can take a wide variety of legal forms, from nonprofit organizations and cooperatives in the social economy, informal groupings based on citizens' groups or rights of use and customs based on other traditions, such as the "Indigenous commons," which have a very different relationship to territory, culture and nonhuman forms of life. The commons is in fact a general principle that can take on a variety of forms with astonishing plasticity: subsistence commons (communal lands, forests, rivers); immaterial commons (free software, Creative Commons, Wikipedia); traditional ecological knowledge; civic and social commons (complementary currencies, local exchange systems); global commons (Antarctica); and so on.[16]

In this sense, we must distinguish this idea of the commons from the abstract idea of the "common good" (which is more synonymous with justice or the general interest) or things like air, oceans or education that appear as "de facto commons." The commons are institutions, that is, a way of regulating practices through common rules that must be instituted. The commons are not inert things but collective practices that come to life through commoning and ongoing forms of cooperation. The common thus combines three elements: (a) a shared good or resource, (b) a community of participants bound by rights of use and obligations and (c) a set of collectively defined rules and social norms for managing the common. The commons, as a global alternative to private and state ownership (promoted by both social democracy and state communism), is therefore very close to the "third way" of self-management socialism.[17]

The commons thus offer a number of advantages: they are both ecological and democratic, they are versatile and modular (favoring institutional pluralism rather than a wall-to-wall approach) and they present a structural alternative to capitalism by outlining the contours of a new economic system. Indeed, the commons can provide a robust basis for the production, distribution and consumption of goods and services in a host of sectors: primary (natural resources, agriculture); secondary (distributed industries); tertiary (collaborative services); and quaternary (culture, care, education, health). The commons can revolutionize both the infrastructure (property relations, productive forces) and the superstructure (political and legal institutions, culture, ideas and values). Philosopher Michel Bauwens has begun to theorize a transition based on the commons and peer-to-peer logic in an effort to socialize the collaborative economy and lay the foundations for a postcapitalist society.[18]

Building postgrowth societies

Another perspective that can be combined with democratic economic planning and the commons is the approach of "degrowth." While the "sustainable development" paradigm has taken off since the 1990s, capturing the collective imagination through a series of discourses, devices, public policies and educational curricula, some authors have pointed out that this worldview contributes above all to greening capitalism and reconciling the irreconcilable: infinite economic growth and ecological sustainability. Authors such as Serge Latouche in France and Jason Hickel in the UK argue that the only possible way to counter global warming and pave the way for just and sustainable societies is to collectively limit the production of goods, energy consumption and the use of natural resources to establish a "no-growth" or "steady-state" economy capable of ensuring shared prosperity.[19]

The essential problems with the growth imperative are not only related to the planetary limits of the economy (infinite growth in a finite world is impossible) but also rising social inequalities, the decoupling of material accumulation and well-being and forms of alienation related to consumerism, productivism, imperatives of performance and social acceleration. These problems are linked to the capitalist mode of production but can also arise in "noncapitalist" countries such as the former Soviet bloc, China and other countries that have taken the path of modernizing industrial societies. Classic left-wing, socialist and communist governments have taken for granted the idea that economic growth, the increase of GDP and development is conducive to wealth and well-being, ignoring the fact that it might be a better strategy to produce fewer but better products, consume less and have more free time, downscale the use of energy and foster resilience at the local level. As sociologist Yves-Marie Abraham points out, degrowth boils down to three principles: produce less, share more, decide together.[20]

Complementary to the notion of degrowth (which puts the emphasis on the critique of the growth worldview), the term *postgrowth* is increasingly used to refer to a future society that could function without submitting to the imperative of unlimited growth in production and consumption. This does not mean that postgrowth implies a systematic reduction in GDP, nor that such a society would be incapable of development or innovation. It's less a question of negative growth (equivalent to an economic recession) than of a society that would be able to make certain sectors grow or shrink according to democratically chosen social and environmental goals. Our societies would no longer be based on a mode of "dynamic stabilization" forcing them to go faster and faster to stay in place (like a hamster running in a wheel) but on an "adaptive" stabilization mode open to initiatives and changes that meet social needs while respecting the planet's limits. As philosopher Hartmut Rosa points out:

> Post-growth society refers to a social formation that has outgrown the dynamic stabilization mode, which is at any time able to grow, accelerate or innovate in order to transform the status quo in a desired direction (for example, with a view to remedying such and such a shortage or problem), but which is not compelled (or condemned) to grow in order to maintain its institutional status quo and ensure its structural reproduction.[21]

Indeed, building postgrowth societies might be the ultimate goal of a new paradigm based on economic democracy, democratic planning and the commons. Some authors combine ideas from the commons and degrowth.[22] A famous young Japanese scholar, Kohei Saito, even argued for the transition to a "degrowth communism" in a best-seller that sold over 500,000 copies during the COVID-19 pandemic. His two books, *Marx in the Anthropocene* and *Slow Down: The DeGrowth Manifesto*, claim that we must distinguish between a productivist, Eurocentric and growth-oriented approach to socialism (like in the Soviet Union) and an alternative pathway to build a "society of the commons" based on radical abundance, the reduction of labor time, local decision making and mutual aid. Saito insists that, "in fact, Marx's version of communism did not aspire to Soviet-style one-party rule and nationalization. Rather, communism was, for Marx, a way to bring about a society in which producers shared the means of production, managing and operating them together as a form of commons."[23]

That being said, it's true that the word *communism* is a loaded term associated with Marxism–Leninism and totalitarian regimes of the last century, where the state played a major role in organizing production with centrally planned economies. This is why we need to not fall into semantic debates and rigid interpretations of the past and to foster new discourses that evoke more positive views of the future such as economic democracy, postgrowth, resilient communities and collective autonomy.

While it is not possible here to enter into all of the exciting debates over the contours of the postcapitalist world, what we can retain is that we can develop concrete alternatives now that can then serve as a basis for changing society. "What we need, then, is 'real utopias': utopian ideals that are grounded in the real potentials of humanity, utopian destinations that have accessible waystations, utopian designs of institutions that can inform our practical tasks of navigating a world of imperfect conditions for social change."[24]

9

Doing business differently

Portrait of an entrepreneur

Putting in place concrete initiatives to change the world requires the involvement of creative people capable of evaluating risk, going off the beaten track and taking new directions, convincing partners, mobilizing resources and starting realistic and viable projects that can bring about social change. The figure of the *entrepreneur* emerges here, the actor who starts a new, value-creating enterprise.

While the word *entrepreneur* has a broader meaning of "project initiator," it is heavily loaded with symbolism and associated with well-known characters of the 19th and 20th centuries such as Thomas Edison, Henry Ford, Walt Disney and John D. Rockefeller or emblematic figures of our own era like Bill Gates, Mark Zuckerberg, Oprah Winfrey, Jeff Bezos, Elon Musk, Jack Ma, Larry Page, Sergey Brin or, closer to home, the Desmarais family, Pierre Karl Péladeau and Guy Laliberté. But can this pantheon of celebrities of the economic world serve as inspiration to people motivated to change society from a social justice perspective? While certainly creative and influential, they are (mostly) men mainly driven by personal ambition who have succeeded in building empires by creating capitalist enterprises geared toward growth and maximization of profits.

This approach seems leagues away from the self-organization of local communities, projects organized by women and immigrant communities, collective action and social protest movements or even the management of small businesses.[1] What is the place of entrepreneurship in a book on social innovation? How can it represent a real tool to change the world? Let's look at the roots of the word *entrepreneur* to throw light on this question.[2] In 18th-century French society, three "orders" or social groups were differentiated: the clergy, the nobility and the "third estate," which compised the great majority of people, including the bourgeoisie. According to economist Richard Cantillon, the bourgeoisie comprised three large groups, "owners, meaning people of independent fortune; farmers; and entrepreneurs, i.e., merchants, manufacturers and lawyers."[3]

Unlike the great merchants of the mercantilist era, who were primarily concerned with trading goods that had already been produced, industrial entrepreneurs had to invest their capital in productive activities to create new products. The economist Jean-Baptiste Say was the first to come up with a precise definition of the industry entrepreneur as someone "who undertakes to create, for his own account, for his own profit and at his own risk, any product."[4] This definition reflects the traditional image of the individual starting up a risky business to launch new goods or services on the market to make a profit.

The idea of novelty, risk and creation play a central role here. An influential economist on the global stage, Joseph Schumpeter, considers entrepreneurs to be real *innovators*, passionate actors whose adventurous spirit is at the heart of economic development, capable of overthrowing routine to carry out innovation.[5] These innovations can take the form of "new products, new procedures, new ways of organizing work, or new uses of existing products."[6] Unlike managers who content themselves with managing an existing company or profiteers who seek to enrich themselves by making their assets and inheritance grow, the entrepreneur is often anticonformist, dynamic and visionary, capable of sparking technological revolutions and "disruptive" innovations that can have immense repercussions on the economic world, social relations and ways of life.

Henry Ford comes to mind: he transformed the processes of industrial production and democratized the sale of cars, thus reshaping the dynamics of urbanization and the way of life for the middle classes. More recently, Steve Jobs shook up the world with the commercialization of the iPhone, accelerating the mass spread of smartphones. Digital platforms like Facebook and X, formerly Twitter, have profoundly changed media, advertising, politics and human relationships. Finally, in the intersection of the sharing economy and digital innovation, enterprises like Uber and Airbnb disrupted the transportation and tourism market with innovative business models.[7]

These diverse processes of "creative destruction" theorized by Schumpeter highlight the central role of innovations and technologies of rupture that shake up the social world, generating crises and eliminating jobs but at the same time creating new possibilities and the strong dynamics of growth behind economic progress.[8]

The figure of the *entrepreneur hero* is very much present in the world of social innovation, heavily influenced by the imagination of start-ups and Silicon Valley. This model, however, tends to conceal certain important aspects such as the strong concentration of wealth in the hands of the big companies, the effects of financial speculation tied to innovations with strong growth potential and the deepening social inequalities that can result. It is also noteworthy that the great majority of entrepreneurs – whether from South or North – do not set up multinationals with explosive growth but individual or family businesses or companies with fewer than 99 employees. In 2023, there were 1.19 million small businesses out of a total of 1.2 million businesses in Canada. These small businesses represented 97.8 percent of all companies in the country and supplied 46.8 percent of jobs.[9]

It is also important to keep in mind that while entrepreneurs do participate in the creation of value through their ideas and their work, the value is created by the human labor and social cooperation of thousands of people who contribute to setting up, organizing, promoting and spreading innovations on the marketplace. In the same way that one person alone would have difficulty producing a simple toaster, whose production relies on collective intelligence and a very complex division of labor, it seems fairly reductive to attribute the creation of wealth to a single individual, however much of an innovator they may be.[10] Especially when, in the market, the new ventures that are the most successful are those started and grown by entrepreneurial teams.[11]

The entrepreneur as a social change actor

Of course, it would be a bit of a caricature to immediately set aside the figure of the capitalist entrepreneur primarily seeking to gain wealth by giving their ideas free rein. The entrepreneur can play numerous roles in society, whether by stimulating local economic development and job creation, participating in social and cultural development through philanthropy or other contributions to the community or through fostering social cohesion and the empowerment of marginalized or disadvantaged groups, as in immigrant entrepreneurship. In short, the classic entrepreneur can have a positive impact on the community, even though their activity is primarily geared toward economic development, growth of their company and profit.

In the 1980s, with Bill Drayton's creation of the Ashoka Foundation, which sought to redefine the role of the entrepreneur, the game-changing notion of "social entrepreneur" emerged. The latter does not simply aim at economic development through the creation of industrial and technological innovation but seeks to resolve social problems and have a positive impact on the community. As we saw in Chapter 1, the social entrepreneur represents a hybrid model, situated between the classic entrepreneur and the social change actor. These two figures are distinguished from each other by the relative weight each gives to their social mission and to the creation of economic value, by their motives and by the profile of the people involved, among other things. Table 9.1 presents a schematic comparison of these two profiles.

We note that the social entrepreneur is, in the first place, distinguished by the centrality of the social in their approach, with economic gain remaining peripheral or parallel. Their posture nevertheless resembles that of the classic creative entrepreneur, as a visionary and one focused on solutions, even though there is an added desire to change the world through the creation of a business that is both profitable and humane.

In Canada, social entrepreneurship has been in vogue for several years, a point Jean-Marc Fontan makes clear:

> In fact, numerous organizations, including private foundations and university centers, are now working on

the development of social enterprise or socioeconomic leadership. These include the Muttart and McConnell Foundations, the Fraser Valley Centre for Social Enterprise, the Sprott Centre for Social Enterprises, the Canadian Centre for Social Entrepreneurship and Enterprising NonProfits.[12]

The goal of these organizations is to support social entrepreneurs by providing tools, methods and capital to drive ideas with strong social impact potential.

The social economy enterprise is not the preferred model in social entrepreneurship circles, which are more interested in *private enterprises with a social purpose* and market activities by nonprofit organizations. Social enterprises are very diverse, emerging from a variety of schools of thought from corporate social responsibility to Muhammad Yunus' social business and the school of market resources, which aims to make nonprofits more financially independent. Since the 2010s, a multitude of social enterprises have shown, for example, the potential of technology for sustainable and responsible development with great social and societal impact. Technological advances enabled the Bibak

Table 9.1: A comparison of classic and social entrepreneurship

	Classic entrepreneurship	Social entrepreneurship
Social mission	Peripheral	Central
Value creation	Maximization of profit central	At same time as fulfilling mission, aims at financial autonomy
Change agent	Innovate for economic development	Innovate to meet social needs
Opportunity	Take advantage of business opportunities on the market	Take advantage of opportunities for social progress
Profile	Risk taking, innovation, engaged in projects, achievement through financial gain	Risk taking, innovation, engaged in projects, achievement through financial gain, plus a desire for social progress, sensitivity to social problems

Source: Roy et al, 2016

company to develop antipersonnel mine detectors for use in Afghanistan in 2015.[13] More recently, the development of drones has enabled the company Dendra Systems to plant trees more quickly and more cheaply in heavily deforested areas, combating widespread clear-cutting in regions such as South Africa and the Amazon. Neopenda is successfully improving newborn care in resource-constrained hospitals through the use of a low-cost, low-power sensor, which has already been deployed in Uganda, Africa, for example. Babyloan has used digital platforms to create an international microcredit institution, enabling citizens around the world to finance social projects in disadvantaged regions. Finally, at a time when 2 billion people have no access to drinking water, Quebec-based Oneka has developed a seawater desalination system that emits no greenhouse gases and requires no energy source.[14]

The plurality of forms of social enterprise, to some extent, blurs the distinction between the private and nonprofit sectors, between big companies seeking social legitimacy and small private businesses with a social mission at the heart of their project. One possible strategy to ensure that the human remains central to the organization is to rely on collective entrepreneurship.[15] The latter arises from the social and solidarity economy (SSE), which emphasizes the *collective* ownership of enterprises (co-ops, nonprofit), noncapitalist allocation of surplus and democratic governance.

The difference between social entrepreneurship and collective entrepreneurship is illustrated, for example, by the criticisms articulated from each side. Social entrepreneurs tend to criticize the social economy over the alleged inefficiency of collective decision making, the inability to have large-scale impact and for overemphasizing the legal status of the enterprise, which does not guarantee its social purpose. On the other side, proponents of the social economy decry the sacrifice of democratic governance for enlightened leaders, having social solidarity reduced to the market and the false claim that social entrepreneurship is new, given that social objectives have been integrated into economic projects in the social economy for a very long time.[16] Before moving on to how to begin a social organization, let's take a look at an example of a very popular alternative organizational structure: the cooperative.

SSE case example: the cooperative model

Often seen as an alternative way to fuel social ambition and business, the cooperative model – along with other SSE models – can best be described as a democratic governance structure motivated by member participation with a collective vision.[17] According to the International Cooperative Alliance, cooperatives are "people-centred enterprises jointly owned and democratically controlled by and for their members to realize their common economic, social and cultural needs and aspirations."[18] In fact, cooperatives around the world share the same seven principles:

1. Voluntary and open membership
2. Democratic member control
3. Member economic participation
4. Autonomy and independence
5. Education, training and information
6. Cooperation among cooperatives
7. Concern for community[19]

Co-ops range from small local shops to large multinational organizations and can be structured as consumer cooperatives, producer or worker cooperatives or even multistakeholder cooperatives involving different types of members. Beyond the most common services (food retail and supply, banking and housing), co-ops have taken the form of services and products, including alternative and community monies, fair trade networks, transportation services and so much more.

One interesting and successful example is the Mondragon Corporation in Spain, which is often cited as one of the world's largest co-ops.[20] The Mondragon model is an association of around 95 autonomous cooperatives owned by their members. Among these co-ops are schools, a grocery chain, catering, research and development tech centers and a consulting firm. Together, their network recorded 11 billion euros in revenue in 2021.[21] Each cooperative has a General Assembly of all members, as well as an elected Governing Council, which oversees the actions of the general manager and various departmental managers.

From the Mondragon governing structure, we can begin to see how power is shared. While the arrangement is far from perfect – much of the authority still forms around individual member cooperatives – many of the larger discussions happen through coordinating, negotiating and facilitating ideas among managers. There are elements of accountability that occur, as well as democratic representation of members in leadership roles. In a sense, this type of arrangement is not only opposed to hierarchical control but relies heavily on coordination among the various units who are embedded in their work and often have a better understanding of their work sectors. In short, Mondragon is an interesting example of how even a flatter, alternative SSE model might work in a market-based system.

How to start a social organization

Beyond the divergences of form and purpose, which set classic, social and collective entrepreneurship apart from each other, they all share the same *process* the entrepreneur or "project leader" must undertake to set up an organization producing goods or services. For social and collective enterprises, the social purpose of the activities and products becomes the priority, and the goal of maximizing *profitability* is replaced with the goal of financial *viability*, to ensure the project lasts. Doing business "otherwise" means setting up economic organizations that place the human, the community and the planet at the center of their concerns.

A new social organization is typically launched in stages. First, the project has to be clearly defined, and it must meet a real social need. It is crucial to carry out an in-depth study of the context, to consult the groups affected (if they are not already involved), to check if other organizations are already addressing this need and to precisely identify the *causes* of the problem the project seeks to address (building on the process identified in Chapter 3). Unlike the classic entrepreneur, who seeks business opportunities and competes with other enterprises, the social innovator must try to meet needs unsatisfied by the market and institutions as well as establish ties of complementarity and collaboration with other social organizations. The primary objective of social innovators, as the Élisabeth-Bruyère School of Social Innovation sees it, is to transform a situation to increase the power of affected individuals and groups to act.

Once the need is confirmed, a team of competent and motivated people with complementary expertise, talents and resources must be formed to take the project forward. Many people like to think about and denounce world problems or get involved from time to time to support a cause, but a social innovation project requires a good deal of perseverance and long-term commitment. It requires knowing how to carry out an idea and develop it into the model of a social organization or even a *business model* in the case of economic organizations with a commercial side.

A social or collective enterprise project requires, among other things, a careful study of the market and the environment. This is mainly to analyze competition (organizations that respond to the same needs and can become future partners), to get a good grasp of market constraints and to identify targeted clients, beneficiaries and potential partners. This indispensable step helps ensure the organization achieves optimal positioning in its environment and increases its chances of success and positive impact. Other elements can contribute to a successful launch, such as getting letters of support from future beneficiaries or clients.

Once the model is constructed, it must be integrated into a *business plan*. This allows the multiple parts of the project to be incorporated and simultaneously addresses several objectives. In terms of external relations, it helps demonstrate the economic viability and relevance of the social innovation project and convince potential partners and funders. Internally, it helps to build a viable model and set clear and measurable objectives and to guide project management. In short, it is an essential tool, both looking ahead at funding applications and for launching the social organization in a good way. Numerous adjustments will be made as the plan is developed: starting hypotheses may shift according to budget projections, the business model could change depending on the analysis of competition and governance could be expanded to include a larger number of players in the organization's strategic decision making.

Funding for the (pre)launch must then be secured. We can observe that social innovations generally draw on hybrid resources: public and private grants, donations, sponsors, members' dues, sales, loans, in-kind contributions such as volunteering, loans of offices and tools, sharing of expertise and so on. Using hybrid resources reduces project costs because of partnerships with other organizations and institutions or community mobilization.

Governments and banks are unlikely to support this kind of project; an innovative strategy to compensate is the use of new funding tools. For example, crowdfunding is often used as a springboard for social innovation projects. Community bonds, for their part, allow community members to buy debt security issued by a nonprofit to help sustain an organization they care about, such as the Grand Costumier and Cinéma du Parc.[22] Social innovation projects are increasingly adopting creative funding strategies, soliciting partnerships with cities or relying on unusual collaborations. The Centre for Social Innovation in Toronto used the community bond model to fundraise the CAD$2 million needed to purchase a new building site.[23] The Community Economic Development Investment Funds in Nova Scotia enable community members to invest in local economic development in their own communities.[24] The collective enterprise Thèsez-vous,[25] which organizes writing retreats for graduate students, decided to open a shared workspace for writing in Montreal and to partner with universities to make its services affordable and to reach the greatest number of students possible.

A new generation of social and collective entrepreneurs is emerging, creating new types of enterprises inspired by a social mission based on a sustainable business model and intending to have a positive impact on the community.

Measuring social impact

There is, however, a trap that many project leaders and entrepreneurs within the field of social innovation fall into: measuring social impact. New tools to evaluate the direct and indirect effects of social innovations over the short or long term are increasingly used as criteria for funding projects. A range of methods and indicators have thus emerged to ensure a supposed "objective" measure of the concrete impacts of an organization: cost–benefit analysis, the Demonstrating Value project, the Global Reporting Initiative, the

Impact Reporting and Investment Standards catalog, social return on investment, evaluation of social utility, to name but a few.

This imperative has preoccupied social innovation circles to such an extent that social and collective entrepreneurs must now integrate social impact into their business model, plan a strategy around it and gear their project toward its potential impact before it has even been launched. Where does it come from? A growing number of organizations (foundations, private investors, governments and intermediary organizations and so on) have endorsed *social finance*, that is, new forms of investment aimed at creating a *measurable* social impact in addition to financial returns.[26] As we mentioned earlier, what we see here are tools and methods being imported from the financial sector into the field of philanthropy and the nonprofit sector, reflecting an approach of philanthrocapitalism.

The generalization of social impact measurements involves many risks. First, the performance indicators can lead some organizations astray from their social mission and initial objectives to reorient their activities according to their effects as measured by the assessment tools. Standardized measurements can also contribute to increasing competition among social enterprises and organizations and can encourage a kind of conformism among social innovation actors, shaping their project to fit evaluation criteria to maximize their chances of getting funding – which runs counter to the very essence of innovation.

Moreover, a lot of time, energy and money is put into systematically measuring the impact – data collection, the monitoring of indicators, accounting, continuous evaluation and so forth – resources that could have been used to pursue the organization's mission and the growth of its positive impact on the community. Here's another paradox: an excessive focus on social impact *measurement* can harm the *real impact* of social innovation.

Finally, it can generate the phenomenon of "business-washing," in which social impact is adopted as a communication strategy, creating a facade concealing negative impacts or the insignificance of changes introduced by an organization.[27]

This said, social impact evaluation methods can also prove extremely useful in some cases. For example, a process of reflection on social impact can meet diverse needs, such as evaluating the relevance of an intervention, continuous improvement of activities and processes of organization and mobilizing the community and project partners. What must be avoided is the reduction of impact measurements to standardized or strictly quantified indicators or to measures of control imposed from the outside to benefit funders. Social organizations must be able to appropriate and define evaluation tools that allow them to increase their social impact according to their mission. As the Montreal Declaration on evaluation and social impact measurement states:

> A good evaluation is an evaluation that will be useful to the organization that is evaluated and those it intends to serve through its activities. A rigorous evaluation must be participatory, collaborative and involve all stakeholders concerned with the process ... The needs and interests of the funders should not take precedence over those of other stakeholders, including producers and users of goods and services. Investments in the social economy must not make it dependent on impact measurement in order to repay investors, as is the case with social impact bonds.[28]

As we can see, there are numerous challenges to launching a collective enterprise and doing business otherwise. Social innovation takes place in a world shaped by the market economy, competition, the imperatives of efficiency and performance, project funding, social impact measurements, standards associated with private enterprise and other constraints that influence its activities, the possibilities for intervention and its internal functioning. Beyond its social purpose and the desire to change the world, social innovation is subject to considerable pressure to conform to the classic private enterprise, from which it is generally distinguished by one key aspect: a mode of functioning based on horizontality, self-management and democratic governance.

10

Organizing democratically

Deconstructing the myth of efficient verticality

Social innovation consists of experimenting with different models, doing business otherwise and developing new organizations outside traditional forms of the economy. But beyond theory, how is this achieved? Often, collective experiments are called utopic because of their claims to horizontality, to functioning without a strict hierarchy. This perception feeds the idea that an organization needs to be led by professional managers or executives to be efficient, while self-management is a chaotic and burdensome process, ultimately doomed to failure. This reproduces the myth of verticality as a gauge of efficiency and democratic horizontality as impossible.

However, it has to be recognized that large companies, just like small businesses and public administration, are fraught with conflict, power plays, technical failures, crises of governance and harassment cases, not to mention generating their share of professional burnout and depression. No organization, hierarchical or democratic, can escape internal conflict, human resources management problems and all kinds of dysfunctionality.[1]

There are currently many horizontal organizations based on mutual aid, cooperation and solidarity: collectives, grassroots committees, social economy enterprises, affinity groups, collegially managed teaching departments, to name but a few. At the same time, an increasing number of large businesses viewed as symbols of performance and efficiency are adopting practices of collaborative management and new organizational models inspired by sociocracy, liberated companies, self-governance and so on.[2]

Taking the example of sociocracy, a concept developed by the Dutch engineer Gerard Endenburg, which combines cybernetic principles and practices inspired by the Religious Society of Friends (Quakers), such as consensus decision making, the use of "circles" to foster small group discussions, "double-linking" to facilitate communication between circles without a top-down hierarchy, as well as "candidate-less elections," which allow everyone to propose a candidate they believe capable of fulfilling a particular role. Although sociocracy remains compatible with a private enterprise structure and is removed from strict self-management in that it maintains a "hierarchy of circles," it nevertheless allows for a certain equality of speech and greater inclusion of members in a shared project. Indeed, many mainstream models of effective management are aligned with horizonal models in emphasizing the importance of active member participation in an organization's strategic decisions. In fact, people feel more motivation and more easily mobilized to accomplish a meaningful activity than simply carrying out a series of tasks.

It is important to note that these new techniques of collaborative management seem to have appropriated 1970s countercultural critiques of the hierarchical organization of labor, surveillance and conformism of the old models of management. As sociologists Luc Boltanski and Eve Chiapello emphasize, the "new spirit of capitalism," inspired by critiques from activist and art scenes, has taken on board aspirations to autonomy, authenticity, creativity and self-fulfillment, with management methods that encourage employee initiative and responsibility and small group collaboration to increase productivity and buy-in to the company's success.[3]

By adopting aspects of self-management, the classic private enterprise grants some autonomy to employees but does not challenge ownership rights or the unequal distribution of surplus. Furthermore, it is clear that a horizontal organization of labor is no less effective and productive. The collective organization of workers without a boss as an intermediary is increasingly seen as an inspiring model, creative and productive for large and small companies alike. While these organizational forms are still in a minority relative to the traditional hierarchical model, this is not because they are less efficient. The view of humans as inherently selfish is so deeply ingrained that it becomes difficult to see self-management as anything but inefficient.

At its core, self-management seeks to bring people together to work equitably on a common project. This model of functioning can be adapted to the varying needs of the organization and the people who comprise it, resolving crises or evolving according to the demands of the society around it. For example, self-management can take the form of a policy of wage equality, including additional revenue for people with dependent children and primary caregivers. This way of functioning also involves redefining responsibilities when a new person arrives, to take into account new skills in the team and the needs of older members for change. The organization, in this way, adapts to humans rather than forcing them to conform to rigid structures supposedly necessary for the proper functioning of the business.

To decenter our gaze and open our imaginations, we can draw on a rich tradition offered by feminist theories in their analysis of power relations within organizations. The ethic of care shows, among other things, that models of interaction based on authority, hierarchies of status and the supposed independence of individuals neglect significant dimensions, such as thoughtfulness, distribution of power and the interdependence of people who share a workspace.[4] Some scholars and practitioners also propose a review of management practices through the lens of care,[5] while others suggest applying activist anti-oppression methods to social enterprises.[6]

Self-management is inspired by a plurality of approaches to challenge the traditional hierarchical model, which is almost systematically presented as the norm, the default option, the best way of ensuring productivity and maximizing organizational performance. The goal is to foster collective autonomy, collaborative work based on reciprocity and shared responsibilities to create another society. Are there practical experiences we can draw on to avoid reinventing the wheel?

A short history of self-management

Fortunately, people aspiring to work without a boss can benefit from a rich heritage. Recent anthropological studies have shown that democracy emerged within multiple communities and societies throughout history, far beyond its supposed birthplace in Athens in the 5th century BCE. Beyond the political regime of the state, it can take different forms: small communities on Madagascar's borders, pirate boats, Iroquois confederations, medieval Icelandic villages, self-managed work collectives and many others.[7]

Historically, the first to theorize self-management were anarchists like Pierre-Joseph Proudhon and Peter Kropotkin, who argued that a propensity to mutual aid is a key factor in the evolution of living species and human societies.[8] The labor movements of the 19th century abound with such experiences: autonomous work collectives, cooperatives, phalansteries, work mutuals and revolutionary experiences such as the Paris Commune of 1871.[9] In the 20th century, the first moments of the Russian Revolution (1905–17) and the Spanish Revolution (1936) were witnesses to vast experiments in self-management. In the summer of 1936, the self-management imaginary and revolutionary syndicalism promised by the National Confederation of Labor led to the collectivization of large swaths of the Spanish economy (industries, services, agriculture), which came under the sole control of workers' collectives.[10]

Closer to us, we saw a new flourishing of self-management in the 1960s and 1970s. The popular uprisings of May 1968, the influence of the Students for a Democratic Society in the United States, the Yugoslavian model of decentralized socialism during the Tito regime and the slogans from the Confédération française démocratique du travail (Democratic French Labor Confederation) and the Parti socialiste unifié (Unified Socialist Party) all helped fuel an age of self-management.[11] During this period, self-management was not just conceived as a way of giving initiative back to employees of a company but as a *political project* explicitly aiming to transform society. The LIP watch-making company, taken over by workers in 1973 in France, and the Tricofil textile factory, taken over by its employees in 1975 in Quebec, are two symbols of an era in which self-management made it possible to overcome the capitalism/state communism dichotomy.

There were numerous other experiments, including the creation of housing cooperatives, self-managed daycares and community-based clinics. More recently, there has been a new wave of self-managed organizations, including the Touski Restaurant and the Euguélionne feminist bookstore in Montreal's Centre-Sud neighborhood and bicycle delivery cooperatives such as CoopCycle in France.[12] There are even some entirely self-managed towns such as Marinaleda in Andalusia, a commune of 3,000 people functioning on direct democracy principles since 1979.

Juan Manuel Sánchez Gordillo, the mayor of Marinaleda from 1979 to 2023, was repeatedly re-elected and still maintains a lot of influence in the community, yet his role as mayor was unpaid, and he worked, like most other people, in the town's farming cooperative. All important decisions about taxation, housing, work and infrastructure are voted on directly by the citizens in general assemblies (100 per year), the mayor playing more the role of spokesperson than the leader of the town.[13]

Numerous intentional communities, otherwise known as "hippy communes," have also been founded. Some of these communities still exist, such as Twin Oaks in Virginia, Findhorn in Scotland and the self-managed Christiania neighborhood of Copenhagen. Other experiences, like the ZAD (zone à défendre) at Notre-Dame-des-Landes, France, recently subject to repression by the Macron government in 2012 and 2018, are similar to the Larzac struggle, where peasants rose up against the occupation of their lands for several years starting in 1971. All of this interest shows that the idea of self-management remains very much alive in our times.

This is even more obvious in contexts of crisis, where self-management seems less of a political ideal than an imperative for survival. Take, for example, the 160 factory takeovers by workers in Argentina at the height of the crisis in 2001.[14] Many self-management projects are now making their appearance in Greece, Spain and Italy, in reaction to the deterioration of the conditions of existence caused by neoliberalism. Most of these self-managed collectives have to improvise new ways of working together, without recourse to practical manuals or specific self-management training.

Learning to self-manage

Because self-management is not a method of organization that is taught or broadly practiced in our societies, it requires a certain deconstruction of reflexes acquired through socialization at home, school and work. The school system almost everywhere around the world generally trains individuals to conform to labor market structures, to be permanently marked and evaluated and to follow employers' instructions. Working in a hierarchical organization presupposes the acceptance of a relationship of subordination that does not stop at the doors of the organization or the business. Accepting to be managed by others (hetero-managed) in our workplaces, we are more inclined to consent to dynamics of rivalry and competition, which promote the exploitation of humans and the destruction of the environment.

Fortunately, the self-management tradition has given an important place to training and pedagogy.[15] This is a precious historical and practical heritage for anyone seeking to transform the dynamics of an organization and, ultimately, the functioning of society. If we want to experiment with democracy on a small scale in our workplaces, we must teach ourselves about horizontality and redefine our relationship to the community and nature so that it is no longer founded on control, calculation and domination.

Collectives that have experimented with self-management in the past or are still functioning in this way have produced numerous toolboxes and other resources from which we can glean experiences, tips and advice on how to function otherwise, both democratically and effectively. For example, some guides compile a range of tools, techniques and methods to support the self-management of ecovillages and intentional communities.[16] Other manuals focus on different strategies aimed at improving communication, resolving conflicts and reconnecting after a difficult period.

Beyond these manuals and practical guides, there are many other ways knowledge is transmitted as well as mutual aid organizations that attempt to circulate knowledge and achievements. For example, the Greek factory VIO.ME, taken over by workers in 2013 and supported by the French organization Amis de VIO.ME, is dedicated to promoting solidarity and knowledge sharing among self-management projects.[17] An open center set up in the factory is responsible for documentation and training.[18] Other organizations such as Bâtiment 7 in Montreal, which brought together more than 18 associations and cooperatives in the first phase of the project, explore self-training possibilities by designing their own model of self-management drawing on different methods and expertise in the field. Finally, other organizations, such as the Sociocracy Group, aim to mobilize, support, train and equip organizations to familiarize them with the methods of sociocracy.[19] Thus, there is an entire array of mutual learning, ranging from advice passed on by word of mouth to practical guides and formalized methods and enterprises specialized in supporting democratic governance.

Reflection on self-management also represents an opportunity to respond to calls from antiracist and Indigenous movements, as well as from deaf or disabled people,[20] who do not simply demand superficial adaptations to promote their inclusion in an unchanged society but offer visions of the world in which modes of interpersonal relations, the physical and practical organization of our environments and even our cultural representations are transformed. If horizontality and self-management are to make our organizations more democratic and inclusive, we must decenter our gaze and listen to the demands of people who are excluded, invisibilized and marginalized and who seek to redefine what is necessary for an in-depth transformation of relational dynamics.

Self-management thus provides an opportunity for people of different backgrounds who come up against structures of domination in different ways to learn to build solidarities. Self-management in this way enables us to develop practices guided by a shared concern of opposing oppression in the workplace. Finally, it is necessary to pay attention to the *micropolitical* of groups just as much as the traditional macropolitical[21] because, while liberatory social innovation aims at large-scale social change, it can't be accomplished without a concrete transformation of collective spaces, rendering them more human, egalitarian, inclusive and creative.

11

Community involvement

Popular education and community organization

While promoting the democratic management of collectives and workspaces is absolutely necessary, democracy can't stop at the doors of the organization or the business. To change the world, we must also – especially – reach a larger number of people and be actively involved in the community. You have likely heard the famous quote from Margaret Mead: "Never doubt that a small group of thoughtful, committed, citizens can change the world. Indeed, it is the only thing that ever has." While social change might start with a small group of people, eventually, we're going to need large masses of people engaged in collective action. In the 1960s and 1970s, grassroots and community movements mobilized a set of methods and intervention tools to promote the self-organization of marginalized groups, human rights, local struggles and the creation of economic alternatives in working-class neighborhoods.[1]

In this era, people working in the field of social work and community facilitation were inspired by liberatory approaches, such as popular education inspired by Paulo Freire's pedagogy of the oppressed and community organizing as developed by activist Saul Alinsky.[2] For Freire, emancipation can never be accomplished solo, in small affinity groups or through actions undertaken by an enlightened avant-garde. It must always happen through a broad process of popular education, mixing theory and practice, reflection and action. "No one educates others, no one is educated alone, men educate themselves together through the intermediary of the world," he stated.[3] One of the keys to change is fostering the *consciousness raising* of the masses, which should be facilitated but not led by educators committed to transforming the establishment.

Alinsky developed an original method of community organizing to counter the social disorganization of the working classes and immigrant groups in disadvantaged neighborhoods of Chicago. His strategy was to enter a neighborhood and patiently meet the residents so he could understand the social issues, the problems of daily life and the challenges in the community. In his view, the starting point to change cannot be a political or ideological program but the real world in all its imperfection:

> As an organizer, I start from where the world is, as it is, not as I would like it to be. That we accept the world as it is does not in any sense weaken our desire to change it into what we believe it should be – it is necessary to begin where the world is if we are going to change it to what we think it should be. That means working in the system.[4]

The main goal of the community organization is to strengthen the power of communities to act, a complex process now described as "empowerment." This especially means building connections to promote individual and collective autonomy and taking collective action to concretely improve the conditions of existence of those affected.[5] Breaking free from *power-over*, which consists of dominating, manipulating or reproducing oppression of the other, Alinksy advocates that excluded groups develop the *power to act* to help them move away from apathy, indifference and powerlessness:

> Power is the very essence, the dynamo of life. It is the power of the heart pumping blood and sustaining life in the body. It is the power of active citizen participation pulsing upward, providing a unified strength for a common purpose. Power is an essential lifeforce always in operation, either changing the world or opposing change.[6]

To develop this power to act, Alinsky organized informal meetings, assemblies and public activities where people could express their needs, frustrations, demands and aspirations collectively. This process allowed for the expression of common concerns, the identification of barriers and opponents and finally the adoption of actions to resolve local problems. Rather than starting a huge battle bound to fail, he suggests targeting precise and realistic goals to obtain small victories that could gradually allow affected groups and individuals to regain confidence.

Obviously, this way of politicizing everyday frustrations and re-instilling some degree of fight-back in local communities to foster concrete change is not the only method that exists. As we noted previously, lots of social movements and community organizations have developed their own tactics and strategies to build popular power and influence authority. There is a multitude of awareness-raising, intervention and facilitation techniques: brain-storms, synthesis charts, coffee hours, theater of the oppressed, popular education workshops, community assemblies, neighborhood parties and many others.[7] As Alinsky says: "So the important thing is how to activate people to agitate, to participate: to be clear, to develop the power necessary to effectively fight the status quo and change it."[8]

Broadening grassroots participation

Other than empowerment and community organizing methods, which attempt to stimulate collective action by marginalized groups, governments have introduced new participatory mechanisms to renew local democracy and promote citizen involvement in existing institutions. A host of democratic innovations such as participatory budgets, citizen juries, codesign workshops, consultive surveys and online participatory platforms diversify the repertoire of available tools and give voice to an increasing number of people on issues that affect them.[9]

That said, the enthusiasm for participatory democracy creates some confusion in the vocabulary, goals and tools of participation. As sociologist Marie-Hélène Bacqué and colleagues note:

> Many notions are used to try to describe these developments: urban governance, local management,

new public management, modernization of local management, participatory democracy. They move between the economic, administrative, political and academic fields; in observation mode and prescriptive mode. Efficient management, transformation of social relations, and local democracy interact in a virtuous circle and sketch a new model of public policy characterised by the repositioning of the state, the development of multifaceted partnerships and civil society initiatives.[10]

For this reason, it is best to avoid a superficial, naïve celebration of this "new spirit of democracy."[11] In fact, governments and private businesses do not uncommonly use participation as a tool to construct the "social acceptability" of big, controversial projects.[12] We could even assume that the value placed on the decentralization of power and sharing of decision making with businesses and civil society actors is sometimes aimed at deconstructing the image of the state as guarantor of the general interest and opening the door to diverse forms of privatization. So, how can we tell if participatory measures are fake or sincere, guarantors of the common good or part of a manipulative strategy?

The first and most famous analytical framework for citizen participation is undoubtedly the "ladder of citizen participation" presented by Sherry Arnstein in 1969. It differentiates among eight levels of participation, ranging from "nonparticipation" (manipulation, therapy) and "symbolic cooperation" (information, consultation, appeasement) to actual citizen power (partnership, delegation of power, citizen control).[13]

The determining criterion in this ladder is the influence citizens have on the decision-making process and not the simple fact of their voices being heard. This is already a helpful index to determine whether a participatory mechanism is primarily a matter of informing individuals (information session); collecting testimonies, analyses and memories for a complex plan; or deciding a difficult question, where a local or national referendum could be used.

That said, decision-making power is not the sole criterion to consider. Another important dimension is the quality of democratic deliberation, that is, the capacity of a participatory space to include a diversity of perspectives, to promote healthy communication, to support an exchange of arguments and mutual transformation of opinion.[14] In a world in which public debate is often made difficult by social media, polarization and echo chambers, it becomes essential to build public spaces conducive to discussion, cordial confrontation of contradictory perspectives as well as collective resolution of shared problems.

As Aristotle emphasized with his "two heads are better than one," a democratic process should in principle lead the people who have come together to make good decisions. Democracy is not simply a matter of asserting the will of the people. It also involves the *rational formation* of the general will. Participatory and deliberative democracy can be defined as a process of collective intelligence aiming to build shared wisdom through dialogue.[15] Drawing of lots is now increasingly used in this respect. Participatory mechanisms such as citizen juries and citizen assemblies examining complex issues (such as voting reform and constitutional reform) allow "ordinary citizens" to deliberate on different questions, in small or large groups, with the support of experts and monetary compensation to ensure a favorable context for deliberation.[16] Selection criteria can also be used to promote greater diversity of perspectives and better representation of gender, social class and ethnic origin.

The conclusions of a collective thought process by community members drawn by lot can then be submitted to elected officials or directly voted on by the entire population in a referendum. Other mechanisms also foster large-scale collective intelligence, such as collaborative platforms allowing individuals in the same state to co-draft bills. In sum, a wide range of citizen and institutional innovations are already helping to reinvent democracy beyond traditional mechanisms of representation.[17]

Finally, we can give the example of the participatory budget, which emerged in 1989 in Porto Alegre, Brazil, and has since spread to hundreds of cities in Europe, Asia, Africa, Latin America and North America.[18] The participatory budget, far from a simple consultation on public finances, allows the public to deliberate on local issues and projects, select investment priorities and directly vote on part of the municipal budget through an annual, transparent process. It introduces an aspect of direct democracy into a representative system, thus expanding citizen participation, fostering the inclusion of marginalized groups and promoting social justice.

The participatory budget of Porto Alegre, for example, ensured the healthy management of the municipal budget, increased participation of the working classes, strengthened the legitimacy of public action and redirected significant resources toward the most disadvantaged neighborhoods.[19] Some might see such a project as utopic, but the formula has been adopted even by large cities such as New York and Paris. In Quebec, Saint-Basile-le-Grand has made CAD$200,000 available to residents since 2014, and several other Quebec municipalities recently followed suit with comparable budgets since February 2019.[20]

The example of the participatory budget shows how experiments in democracy can easily emerge at the local level and that municipalities can play a strategic role in supporting and promoting social innovation.

Transforming municipal policy

In the move from local initiatives to large-scale changes, cities are a crucial space to accelerate the transition toward a more ecological, democratic, just and inclusive society. A host of social innovations in the economic, social and environmental fields are emerging in cities around the world: urban agriculture, complementary local money, takeovers of industrial buildings and vacant lots, free public transport, tactical urbanism, active transport infrastructure, climate change mitigation measures, integrated land use planning – the list goes on.

Beyond the "asphalt" view,[21] in which the role of municipalities is limited to garbage collection, snow removal, road repair and potholes, local governments are called upon to play a growing role in economic, social and cultural development and are increasingly responsible for the inclusion of immigrants, health, the preservation of ecosystems, citizen participation and adapting to the aging population. While the financial resources of municipalities are limited and dependent on property tax, which promotes urban sprawl and the increasing influence of private promoters, cities continue to demand ever-greater autonomy to contribute to community resilience and improve the quality of life within their territory.

Innovative land development initiatives are not limited to urban settings but have been launched in rural areas, for example, in the village of Saint-Camille in the Eastern Townships of Quebec. This 500-person community created its own model of local revitalization, combining collective entrepreneurship, shared governance, conversion of a manor into a co-op for the elderly, the transformation of a church into a multimedia conference hall, the twinning of the Saint-Camille women's association with the Dégnékoro commune in Mali, weekly pizza dinners at the local community center and so on.[22] There is also the village of Guyenne in Abitibi, Quebec, which has, for the most part, relied on a radically cooperative model of development since 1947, even formerly being referred to as "little Russia."[23]

All of these scattered initiatives are now starting to converge within a transnational movement to collectively reappropriate local institutions. Municipalism is an emerging grassroots movement and a global project that views the municipality as the main springboard for the democratic transformation of social, economic and political life.[24] Libertarian municipalism, first developed as a theory by US ecologist and philosopher Murray Bookchin,[25] has a long history rooted in experiences of direct democracy and local self-government (the city of Athens, medieval communes, New England town hall meetings) as well as revolutionary moments such as the Paris Commune (1871) and Red Vienna (1918–34).

A new municipal wave has now emerged: Spain's rebel city halls taken over by grassroots platforms in 2015; Kurdish democratic confederalism in the Rojava area of Syria; and the municipality of Jackson, Mississippi, which combines popular assemblies, a federation of self-managed cooperatives and the 2014 election of a new municipal government that emerged from Black liberation struggles.[26] Notably, these diverse experiences of trying to change the world at the local level incorporate an entire constellation of social innovations and elements we have highlighted in this book, including roots in critical perspectives and social movements, effective framing strategies, economic transformation projects, collective entrepreneurship, self-management and broad community participation.

Municipalism is not just about managing the city otherwise but about transforming municipal politics to become an incubator for local innovation and social change. In Barcelona, for example, the city began a *remunicipalization* of some services, such as water and energy (through the creation of the municipal business Barcelona Energía), the establishment of a "civic management" of public goods administered directly by the community through a 30-year use transfer and the launch of the digital platform Decidim Barcelona, which is a free digital democracy and collaboration online program now used by more than 30 cities around the world.

Of course, municipal action can't change everything. Our cities face many obstacles, including neoliberal globalization, which places territories in competition and centralizes power and strategic skills in the hands of nation-states. They must also come to terms with municipal taxation, which makes them dependent on property taxes, and, in Canada, the constitutional constraint that makes their power subordinate to provincial powers. To overcome the structural inferiority of municipalities to states, a transformative city policy must foster solidarities between urban and rural centers, as well as transnational alliances among rebel cities, and carefully consider the question at the heart of social change: How do we move from isolated projects, however inspiring, to a global movement capable of bringing about fundamental, large-scale transformation?

12

Culture as resistance

When we think about social change, many people think spontaneously about changing our values, our culture and our way of life. But what does it mean exactly, in practice? Culture is complex yet ubiquitous. Governments often proclaim the enjoyment of national museums to be a cultural activity. In fact, many governments own and manage museums and art galleries under an official department of culture and have authoritatively established them as "cultural." Once inside, many objects and presentations, arranged thematically, expose visitors to many styles and designs, often requiring a lot of knowledge to interpret and appreciate them. For many art professionals and elites, the ability to recognize and appreciate their beauty is determined by how "cultured" the visitor is, a quality determined by their socioeconomic status and experience.[1] Finally, by visiting thematic exhibits about societies or past communities, visitors are once again informed that these groups had unique cultures that shaped their way of life. So, what exactly is culture and how can people recognize and mobilize it to change the world?

What is culture and why is it important?

According to Welsh scholar and cultural Marxist Raymond Williams,[2] there are three general categories of definition for culture: (a) the "ideal," where "culture is a state or process of human perfection, in terms of absolute values"; (b) the "documentary," where "culture is a body of imaginative and intellectual work in which the highest human values are realised"; and (c) the "social," where "culture is a particular way of life, expressing certain values not only in art and learning but also in institutions and ordinary behavior." Penned in response to a book arguing solely for the first category, culture as an "ideal," Williams wanted to show us that culture carried many meanings that intersected in daily life. The argument that culture should take only one defined form does not accurately represent the term.

From a social innovation perspective, defining *culture* as a way of life that expresses values and norms through a variety of activities and behaviors aligns well with our efforts to socially enhance, empower and change the world around us. With that in mind, this view does put us at odds with the other two categories. First, how can culture be understood as an "ideal" without reinforcing oppressive practices of differences – that is, othering – by suggesting there is only one "ideal type" and anything else is less? How can truth, aesthetics and beauty, morality and an individual's worth be reduced to a single context-free standard? In trying to do so, we would be adhering to a single absolute and ignoring alternative cultures and the value of being different in favor of a "true" or "ideal" culture. Second, how do we determine if an activity is cultural or not? This is a common debate for art and the motivation behind its creation - do we create art for art's own sake or for some other instrumental reason?[3] For similar reasons, we may question what authoritative institutions (government, corporations, networks, for example) might designate an activity as "cultural" versus "not cultural."

By accepting and adopting a broader and more open understanding of culture as a "way of life," we create a more fluid view of how cultures can coexist and navigate our shared existence.

Authority and disempowerment: a culture of oppression

For centuries, culture has been used by the elite and privileged as a weapon to systematically oppress the public. In 16th-century Europe, for example, different cultures were seen as oddities but revered for their difference and rarity. However, this intrigue led to new scientific taxonomies of knowledge that began to structure and reinforce these differences among cultures - along with the negative sentiments and implications - that led to further divisions and increased "othering" in the 17th century. In the late 18th century, established owners of cultural items began amassing and sorting them based on artistic tastes and curiosities to demonstrate royal and family power, prestige and wealth.[4] In doing this, these colonial owners of stolen and appropriated culture used them as instruments of domination to establish a division and authority between the visiting public (the dominated) and the ruling cultural elite (the authority and owners of capital).

In the 1900s, culture circulated out of the hands of most elites and became increasingly instrumentalized by governments. The establishment of the International Council of Museums (ICOM) further established and standardized how culture could be displayed, collected and conserved; however, discussions about inclusive narratives, collections being returned and public participation in how these items would be displayed did not yield much success. Thus, cultural institutions collected objects, and, under the order of many governments - who owned and operated these institutions - these displays continued skewed narratives that did not reflect their roots or communities. Worse, governments oppressively used these spaces to "educate" and "civilize" their visiting public.

In France, for instance, in the early 1960s, Minister of Cultural Affairs André Malraux argued for the importance of national culture and of developing instruments to protect and spread it.[5] For Malraux, it was necessary to create a harmonious idea of an enlightened French high culture that needed to be "shared" with the population at large because he believed people in modern civilization were subject to their "organic" instincts (sex, blood and death), preventing them from embracing a commitment to rationality (scientific thought and laws of the world). To spread this culture, Malraux created houses of culture - structures of reception located throughout France - to disseminate authorized scholarly culture and artistic works to the wider public.

Similarly, in Canada, Prime Minister Pierre Elliott Trudeau and his Secretary of State Gérard Pelletier began putting initiatives in place in the 1960s in support of their cultural vision. Many changes were made with this new vision, including the introduction of the National Museums Act 1968 to reorganize the sector to include permanent crown-owned cultural institutions such as the National

Gallery and several national museums, and the establishment of new museums and financial support. However, Pelletier and Trudeau's vision was not concerned with the representation of the various cultures and traditions of Canadians and, instead, favored a "national cultural heritage."[6] Pelletier acknowledged that museums were vital to how the public viewed itself, its heritage and the broad culture in which it belonged.

While culture has generally been associated with exhibits, performances, galleries and museums, it is important to note it is also present in prisons, hospitals and schools. For Canada, one of the worst examples of cultural assimilation was the cultural genocide inflicted by the residential school system.[7] These schools had the objective to culturally assimilate Indigenous children into Canadian society and were operated in partnership with the Anglican, Catholic, Methodist and Presbyterian Churches. Financed by the Canadian government, the schools operated between the 1870s and the 1990s by forcibly removing Indigenous children (ages four to 16) from their families and communities and forcing them to attend residential schools. To culturally assimilate them, children were forbidden to speak their Indigenous languages and forced into new cultural (English or French language, haircuts or shaved heads, uniforms) and religious practices (prayer, new religious values, vilification of Indigenous values) and tortured (sexual assault, electrical shock, eating spoiled food, starvation, freezing, withholding presents and letters from family and so on). These schools were seen as an effective way to "civilize" Indigenous children.[8]

In sum, culture has been a powerful instrument in the hands of many powerful groups. First, culture and its associated objects and symbols were wielded as symbols of colonial victory, domination and power. Second, appropriated cultures were examined and categorized to demonstrate difference and divide and "other" the public. Finally, culture was repurposed as a way to manipulate and control the public. The most disturbing component these trends and practices reveal is that the public and referenced communities are excluded from cultural decision making. Not only are their cultures, heritages and histories mounted and displayed – often the result of colonial theft and appropriation – but the consent, consultation and affirmation of these cultures, objects and narratives are not reflective of their respective people and communities.

Community empowerment: taking back our culture

The study of culture and how it affects us can offer an account of the ways people use it to socially organize a group of linked values, norms and ideals, and how it is produced and sustained through the assembly of elements.[9] Exploring culture can also reveal relations between culture and power, which cultures are dominant and used as oppressive instruments or how culture is historically reinterpreted and politicized to enforce certain perspectives and narratives on behalf of governments and the elite.[10] Being familiar with how culture can oppress us is important; but understanding how taking back and reinstating culture can be empowering is even more important. For many, culture can be a tool used to oppress; for others, culture is not a means to an end – instead, it is an end unto itself.[11] Culture, in this sense, can illustrate many things.

Since the early 1970s, new movements in the cultural sector began to emerge seeking new ways to repurpose how culture was being used and how cultural institutions, like museums, managed and displayed community heritage. In 1971, a group of cultural activists at the ICOM general assembly in France pushed for changes in these institutions, arguing that they needed to "undertake a continuous and complete reassessment of the needs of the public which they serve."[12] With the idea of "serving the public," new, alternative cultural institutions began to emerge to meet these needs, in confrontation with the ones owned and managed by the elite and government.

One way these alternative cultural institutions have empowered people is through a set of shared values, norms and objectives. For example, in Canada, several laborers, union activists and community members in the city of Ottawa assembled and organized a cultural institute called the Workers' History Museum. Due to their shared militant experiences, together the group declared a shared set of collective values, which includes solidarity, cooperation, honesty, equity, responsibility and fairness. This declaration became a cultural beacon to attract and unite other working people who are interested in participating in a space to gather, socialize, develop and exchange knowledge, outside of any government or elite interference.

Second, these new, reclaimed, cultural institutions can also provide people and the community at large a way to remind us of hard-fought victories and historical struggles. For example, located in Montreal, Quebec, l'Écomusée du fier monde began with locals involved with les Habitations communautaires Centre-Sud (a local resource group devoted to cooperative and public housing, also concerned with the development of the district).[13] The creation of l'Écomusée du fier monde was seen as an answer to a number of different problems that emerged in the Centre-Sud neighborhood in the late 1970s. One of the major, long-standing exhibits created by and for the community is 'À coeur de jour! Grandeurs et misères d'un quartier populaire' – a permanent exhibit that focuses on describing the history of workers, their living environments and the daily strategies they used to make ends meet.[14] Moreover, the narrative was collaboratively created to retell the broader economic history of the neighborhood that was hit hard by deindustrialization, which shaped the destiny of the working classes of Montreal.[15]

Finally, another major role reclaiming a culture can provide is a means to empower its community to change their world and take back its public space. For the Workers' History Museum, this meant "trying to repopulate the commemorative landscape ... [by] show[ing] that we are here, we are present, and that working people's experience needs to populate that landscape."[16] This sentiment is well represented by Montreal-based l'Écomusée de l'Au-Delà. This nonprofit cultural institution promotes knowledge, conservation and restoration of cemeteries and supports initiatives that develop new forms of burial and commemoration of the dead, on behalf of its community of workers, supporters and believers in various spiritual and cultural practices. This focus is the result of the public's waning interest in cemeteries and the commemoration of the dead, which began in the 1940s – after the golden age of funerary art when specialists and commemoration were celebrated.[17] Concerned about yet interested in the funerary heritage of Montreal, citizens formed this cultural institution as a way of reclaiming the pride and celebration of their work and industry. Moreover, citizens were also motivated by their concern for the construction of mausoleums in the Notre-Dame-des-Neiges cemetery, which were seen as potentially affecting the environment because they were incompatible with the concept of the cemetery garden and thus did not meet the criteria for sustainable development.

In sum, when used by communities and locals, culture is a powerful component of everyday life. While the powerful elite may use culture to oppress the vulnerable, communities can remind themselves of how their culture unites them through their shared norms, values and goals. A shared culture is also a good way to inspire, by establishing a record of a people's shared events, struggles and many victories. Finally, instead of using culture as an instrument to harm and assimilate, it can be used by communities as a binding source to empower individuals to take action, form a community and reappropriate their heritage and public space.

Formed in 1991 by several Montreal citizens and activists concerned about funerary heritage, l'Écomusée du patrimoine funéraire et commémoratif (EPFC) draws on an alternative model of museums that is paired with a social innovation objective and a drive to authentically connect with its surrounding ecosystem. More specifically, EPFC presents several institutional elements that are distinctive from public museums. For instance, the ecomuseum presents missions that claim to "work with," "mobilize" and "unite" its various funerary and commemorative communities.[18] Together, these declarations imply an active commitment to its public and environment. More interestingly, these statements reflect a holistic approach to the ecomusuem's relationships, one that is also reflected in its connection to a local sense of "place" (that is, community, nature, heritage), extending well beyond the physical environment (that is, buildings, roads, sites). These claims represent a remarkably different model than public museums whose hierarchy and established managerial roles dictate institutional goals, values, practices and project outcomes. Furthermore, we can see how these characteristics can illustrate more than just an alternative museum approach; instead, they offer a new form of community and an authentic sense of identity and belonging.

Before diving further into the ecomuseum model, we should first understand the classical model of the public museum, which was largely colonial in nature. During the late 17th and 18th centuries, museums took the form of private structures, temples and curiosity collections filled with privately purchased items and the spoils of colonial plunder. In each case, these museums generally served to demonstrate family power, prestige and royalty.[19] Essentially, this presentation of bourgeois status functioned as an instrument of domination that cemented the asymmetric relationship of authority between the public (the dominated) and the ruling cultural elite (the museums and its owners). Reforms reacting to this antagonistic relationship led to heritage works being circulated and reconstituted in the hands of public museums with a desire to make these works more accessible for visitors and communities.

By design, the public museum is a largely exclusive institution. If we turn to the model (see Figure 12.1) as developed by activist and museology expert René Rivard, we can observe the one-dimensional experience the public museum provides. At the heart of this model is the physical structure of the museum. Not only does this building guide and separate the experts and collections from the public it purports to represent but it symbolically reinforces the division of the public and their label as a visitor and consumer. Within the protection of the structure, the most valuable are secured and simultaneously legitimized through their enshrining. In other words, it is the curators and managers that authorize the cultural narratives and chosen displays and assembled collections. Simply put, visitors (the public) come in, are "educated" by the collections assembled by the "experts," then leave. Unfortunately, this process of learning is far from engaged or collaborative in nature. The curators and "experts" that create cultural narratives are often far removed from the context of their objects and collections, which are then stripped of their relationship with the land, heritage and people who use, understand and value them. Ultimately, the public museum model is a narrow and hollow experience focused on the global tourist experience. Consequently, these cultural institutions are often devoid of the actual heritage that grounds these valuable and unique collections.

Figure 12.1: Public museum model

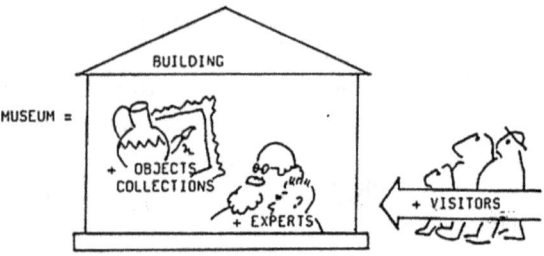

Source: Rivard, 1984

On the other hand, the ecomuseum model, as showcased by Rivard's illustration (see Figure 12.2), is a much more holistic approach to heritage and culture. Originally coined by Hugues de Varine and and developed with the help of cultural and museum scholar Georges Henri Rivière, the term ecomuseum evolved to encapsulate the idea of museums created by local heritage and driven by local communities for community development.[20] While earlier interpretations of the concept fixated on the prefix "eco" and questioned whether ecomuseums should continue to involve an ecological component or not, the model ultimately took form to include nature and environmental quality within its design. Of course, communal and grassroots characteristics remained at the heart of the ecomuseum's function and identity. Interestingly, in Rivière's view of the ecomuseum, it is a mirror of the community and its people; an expression of human and nature and of time; an interpretation of space; and a laboratory, conservation center and school with common principles.[21]

In short, as a cultural institution that is community owned and managed, we already begin to see how this approach differs from the colonial model. As a function, the ecomuseum is multidirectional, without barriers and exclusion. A building is no longer necessary or at the center of the model. People are empowered as public and local experts, eschewing their role as temporary visitors. Similarly, outside experts that may not be traditionally recognized, such as elders, have a space to include their shared experiences and add important heritage context

Figure 12.2: Ecomuseum model

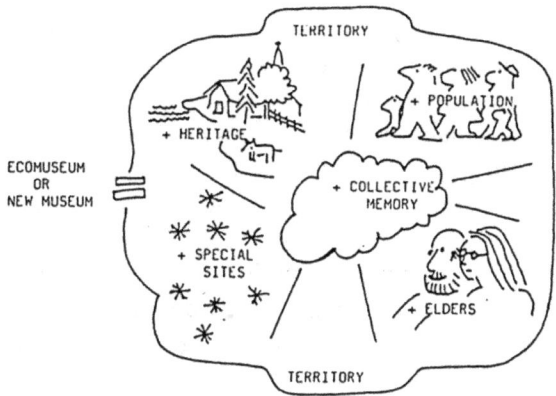

Source: Rivard, 1984

that is usually missing in authenticating items or explaining ceremonies for their use. Nature, territory and the overall sense of place that includes particular sites, areas of heritage, ceremonies and peoples all form a collective memory that represents the idea of a specific ecomuseum project. Despite this amalgamation of "stuff," the ecomuseum's multitude of faces all reflect the same goals: to critically analyze local heritage, foster awareness of the community, promote and broaden local skills and offer insights into the future.

For EPFC, the ecomuseum model has been central to its function and identity. Founded as a nonprofit charity (under the name la Fédération Écomusée de l'Au-Delà), EPFC was initially created in 1991 as an instrument to circulate former president and founder Alain Tremblay's passion and concerns related to death, funeral rituals, representations of the afterlife and the environment.[22] Primarily an influence in the province of Quebec, the ecomuseum was an institution without a physical building. The austerity measures it, along with many other cultural institutions, faced made it nearly impossible to develop, promote or protect the funerary industry in different regions all over Quebec. Thus, with a regional focus in mind, the ecomuseum began to sprawl in various community areas where it created sectional associations of people (region-specific cultural projects) with the same goals as the museum to accomplish its social objectives.

The values and objectives of this alternative model are best explained through EPFC's thematic structure.[23] To understand these thematic pillars, EPFC includes aspects, practices, objects, places, rituals, beliefs, sciences and symbols, each supported by a plethora of broad and inclusive subthemes.[24] In his 30-year retrospective, founder Tremblay outlines the milestones evidenced by many participatory engagements: collaborative publications (journals, self-published); weekly activities and community visits; the creation of new committees, conferences and studies (even one on citizen vigilance for the city of Montreal); policy briefs submitted to the public consultation office; collaboration agreements among many groups (businesses, universities, cemeteries); and coproduced exhibitions.[25] Many of these activities engaged with authors, local business collaborators, university and nonprofit volunteers and benefactors. With this in mind, we can begin to see how a new model might lead to different and expansive practices that are more inclusive of the public and its overall community. Given how dynamic and complex subjects like culture and heritage are, it is necessary to adapt them to their larger networked ecosystem and showcase how culture and its related services are important for, and embedded in, public life.

Culture: a catalyst for a better future?

As more and more individuals and communities begin to recognize the uniqueness and value of their culture, we are seeing increasing attempts to form new cultural institutions as rallying points. In Ottawa, Canada, a new institution, the Vanier Museopark, was inaugurated in 2006. Reflecting the Franco-Ontarian spirit of the neighborhood, the park represents a new legacy of its early heritage and a desire to widely share its identity, its values, its societal contributions and its enduring strength as a people.

In the end, is culture the key to transforming this world and its current neoliberal problems? The answer is not that simple. In the wrong hands, the development of a culture has been used to bind people, their heritage and history, their values and customs, and even their very will to take action. However, when embraced, culture is a beacon that unites under an umbrella of shared norms and goals that remind us of our shared strife and a sense of public and of place.

13

Where do we stand? Unsettling the neoliberal university through engaged pedagogy

In this book, we have offered various tips and strategies to change the world, based on a specific definition of social innovation and a specific analysis of the world and how to change it.[1] As we have seen, the practices and actors that bring life to social innovation exist in all areas of society, in workplaces, community centers and households, from community gardens to massive mobilizations in the streets. Building on the principle that the potential for collective action and social change exists everywhere, we are often encouraged to look no further than our own current surroundings and context. For us, as professors, this involves examining the university as a potential site and driver of social transformation.

Within our school, we have discussed the degree to which the university is, or could be, a meaningful terrain of struggle. Whether emancipatory and liberatory politics are possible within the structures and confines of academic institutions is not something that we all agree on. But one thing we do all agree on is that if university is to be a meaningful site through which social transformation can occur, it begins with a return to pedagogy as central to university everyday life.

To fully explain our position, we must start from the beginning, which for us, is pedagogy. Pedagogy is not just something to be employed inside the four walls of a classroom. For us, pedagogy is deeply rooted into praxis, and it is foundational to the ways we engage with the broader community. And we believe that this reflexive chapter can be addressed to colleagues as well as students. As bell hooks stated, a transgressive pedagogy involves the participation of everyone in the classroom.[2]

Pedagogy occupies, paradoxically, very little space at the university. At least, compared to research: "Most of us are not inclined to see discussion of pedagogy as central to our academic work and intellectual growth, or the practice of teaching as work that enhances and enriches scholarship."[3] This is not altogether surprising, considering the effects of decades of neoliberalization and corporatization of the university, which consistently devalues teaching and pedagogy in favor of research and "innovation."

Despite this, we see great value and importance in reflecting on pedagogy and in seeing it as not only an individual practice but a shared, collective endeavor. bell hooks invites us to reflect on our daily teaching practice by asking a simple question: "How can we serve?"[4] Reflecting upon our teaching and research practice means swimming against the tide by refocusing on meaningful community service. And we believe we must put pedagogy back at the core of our commitment to an engaged learning community.

Engaged research as a response to the neoliberalization of the university

As Jamie Brownlee, scholar and writer on the sociology of education, argues, the entrepreneurial rationality that marked the restructuring of universities has had a significant impact on the direction and priorities of higher education in Canada (and around the globe).[5] Funding for universities is decreasing overall, and universities are facing increasing pressure from the state to adopt more efficient governance models and to pursue private funding for research and academic programs.[6] This has consequences for how professors' work is evaluated, reflected in the allocation of resources as the value accorded to particular types of research. Excellence is reduced to a certain number of quantifiable variables pushing toward the standardization of university models.[7]

Research is taking an increasingly large place in academia.[8] While this is not in and of itself problematic, the following trends most definitely are:

- Research excellence has become the main – and sometimes the only – criterion for advancement in the profession.[9]
- Funding is increasingly directed toward sponsored research.[10]
- Pressure is greater to obtain external funding, to publish quickly and preferably in certain journals.[11]
- The structure of the institution does not support engaged research undertaken in a way that is helpful to the community the research project was organized with.[12]

Furthermore, in recent years, many voices have criticized the alienating and exclusive nature of academia.[13] The conditions created by these many institutional and individual pressures are a far cry from the conditions needed to build and conduct research projects that address issues of social justice and social transformation.[14] There is a lack of institutional recognition of and support for *research with*, a term proposed by sociologist Jean-Marc Fontan et al "to bring together all these forms of connections between academics and non-academics" in research, in particular collaborative research, participatory research, action-research and partnership research.[15] Further, the culture of efficiency bristles against the necessary times and rhythms of the organizations and individuals involved in collaborative, participatory work, undermining its success and rigor.[16]

Beyond the prioritizing of research, teaching is also undermined by the very funding structure of universities. According to Brownlee, the neoliberal restructuring of universities pushes teaching further down the list of priorities.[17] Maximizing the number of "income units" (that is, the provincial funding granted per student) takes precedence over administrative decisions affecting pedagogy. This results in an increase in administrative staff in universities and an increase in the student/teacher ratio.[18] In smaller universities, this manifests in a quest to attract – and keep – students by creating more job-oriented programs, lowering the expectations and/or admitting students even if they do not fully meet the requirements. Students are seen merely as a source of revenue. In the words of hooks: "When professors 'serve' each other by a mutual commitment to education as the practice of freedom, by daring to challenge and teach one another as well as our students, this service is not institutionally rewarded."[19]

All of this is in addition to the increasingly frequent hiring of professors on limited-term contracts with a greater teaching load. In the face of these challenges and constraints, the teacher tends to retreat into their professorial posture, reduce dialogue with students to the extreme and even, sometimes, turn away completely from learning issues in the classroom. It is a model that Paulo Freire described as the *banking model of education*, where the transmission of knowledge is unilateral, formulaic and disembodied.[20] We can say without a doubt that the technological acceleration induced during the COVID-19 pandemic has further entrenched this model, with professors being forced to adopt online, sometimes prerecorded teaching without any prior in-depth preparation. And we know this pedagogic "state of exception" created by COVID-19 has left permanent changes, as this move toward online learning (hence reducing costs of infrastructure and workforce) was pushed by many institutions prior to the pandemic.

Put simply, teachers' investment in their teaching practice is not very strategic – or if it is, it is done according to the neoliberal model (for example, teaching to meet institutional evaluation criteria like favorable student evaluations).[21] In this logic, each effort to serve the community and/or to put the teaching component at the center of our practice has an opportunity cost on research and consequently on career advancement.

Research, therefore, remains that which can provide access to significant capital in the academic field, capital that can be counted in quantitative terms: the number of publications, grants, conferences, symposia and citations. Community-engaged and/or participatory research is no exception to this rule, and researchers who have taken this path will have had to invest much more time in coordination and meetings than their colleagues to meet the same evaluation criteria. Despite this, many make the effort to promote engaged research within their university and succeed in advancing their academic careers. In fact, engaged research represents the most frequent response from academics who want to take concrete action in their communities and their society.

While engaged research is no doubt valuable, it does not disrupt the daily life of academics or the daily functioning of universities.

The focus of most engaged research is external, seeking to have an influence on society, as opposed to the internal practices of universities that maintain and perpetuate many harmful systems. For this reason, we find engaged research to be essential but insufficient as a strategy of resistance to the neoliberalization of the university and its impact on our practices.

Rethinking pedagogy in our daily life

The works of Freire, Mohanty and hooks have been central to our reflections on university practice and the importance of creating and participating in an engaged learning community. Taken together, they outline a vision of radical pedagogy that informs not only our approach to students and the classroom but how we interact and relate with one another. And in doing so, they have influenced our very understanding of social innovation.

Freire

First and foremost, Freire inspires us through his invitation to critically reflect on the practice of teaching, understood as a praxis for social transformation: "Teaching is not about transferring knowledge, but about creating the possibility for its production or construction."[22] As Freire notes, pedagogical praxis involves both action and reflection, not as distinct activities but as inherently linked, each informing the other. Returning to his work allowed us to clarify what is meant by "critical thinking" in an educational context.[23] Freire's method has five components: it is intended to be *inductive* because it is anchored in the immediate reality of the teacher and students; it is *dialogic* because it involves collective discussion; it *problematizes* because it aims to question, criticize and transform society; it is *axiological* because it reveals the features of social conflicts structuring social reality; and, finally, it is *democratic* because, for Freire, "[t]he more critical a human group is, the more democratic and permeable they are."[24] In a nutshell, the classroom is seen as a space of conflict and transformation, where the professor acts as a facilitator of critical knowledge instead of an enforcer of what is right or wrong. Freire's method aspires to move learners (including the teacher) from *object* to social and political *subject* through critical insertion into society.

Mohanty

To make the implementation of an emancipatory pedagogy possible, Mohanty launches a call to "transform our institutional practices fundamentally." This involves:

> the grounding of the analysis of exploitation and oppression in accurate history and theory, [and] seeing ourselves as activists in the academy – drawing links between movements for social justice and our pedagogical and scholarly endeavors and expecting and demanding action from ourselves, our colleagues, and our students at numerous levels.[25]

She invites us to transform our day-to-day living so as to have a significant and direct impact on oppressive dynamics. Mohanty proposes the idea of *making pedagogy*, an effort centered on social action and the establishment of a learning community. Indeed, the systematization and collectivization of resistance within a committed teaching and learning practice allows for greater social effectiveness. Mohanty proposes we make the classroom a space where students develop critical thinking and where we collectively create and disseminate alternative models of teaching and learning.

Such a practice is essential for problematizing the dominant normativity of the academic curriculum. For Mohanty, however, challenging the dominant narrative also involves resurfacing and reappropriating the suppressed histories and knowledge of marginalized communities. This involves decentering the teaching of "classic" authors and questioning the voices considered legitimate. But it also means making room for marginalized voices, to promote their knowledge and experiences by facilitating dissemination and developing collaborations. "To serve" takes the form of an educational redefinition, making alternative stories and knowledge the foundation of a pedagogy centered on emancipatory practices and rooted in the community.

hooks

For hooks, the classroom deserves special attention because it carries a unique potential for thinking and building social transformation: "Education as the practice of freedom is not just about liberatory knowledge, it's about a liberatory practice in the classroom."[26] The classroom constitutes "the most radical space of possibility in the academy."[27] "Education as a practice of freedom" is then made possible by the transgression of borders and ways of thinking and imagining.[28]

As hooks outlines, developing critical thinking also involves going beyond content and rethinking the learning space. Propagating critical thinking makes it possible to deconstruct the way "power has been traditionally orchestrated in the classroom, denying subjectivity to some groups and according it to others."[29] Thus, hooks invites us to question how our practices reproduce systems of domination, to think about and develop new ways of teaching and to put ourselves at the service of students. This involves changing the paradigm, changing how we teach – both the method and the content. A good example presented by hooks is about how our bodies occupy space, how we might feel uncomfortable in a class when we leave the podium or when we transgress the imaginary line that separates us from the group. This example also applies to students, who can be reluctant to choose courses that involve their active participation. A radical pedagogy requires us to dissolve the boundaries that separate the teacher from the students but also the boundaries of students themselves. A classroom that invites the creation of a learning community involves a personal investment from both the teacher and the students. It is a challenging process that involves being vulnerable, questioning our privileges, building relationships and giving an authentic commitment.

From this perspective, it is a question of continually transforming ourselves, bringing to life a praxis of liberation, to "renew our minds ... so that the way we live, teach and work reflect our joy in cultural diversity, our passion for justice and our love of freedom."[30] This transformative process considers both the everydayness and the complexity of our lives. Practicing our work as teachers as a daily effort to generate solidarity and authentic social connections with marginalized communities makes teaching both meaningful and demanding. It requires us to take the time to meet and be in relation with those with whom we build these communities of learning and of practice, to transgress the established power relations, to dismantle oppression and to make room for reflexivity as a fundamental component of our praxis. At its core, it is an exercise of vulnerability, because adopting critical pedagogies requires a strong commitment and an openness to being confronted in one's practice.[31]

How we rethink pedagogy at the Élisabeth-Bruyère School of Social Innovation

Taken together, the ideas of Freire, Mohanty and hooks make it possible to rethink the space of the classroom and to reflect upon its deep links with community service. It also allows us to incorporate care into the relations we have with students, staff and each other. Our collective reflections around these questions led us to develop a very specific educational approach as well as spaces to support it. Our journey has been complex, and we are constantly adjusting; but it seems to us that this path is one of the ways to take pedagogy seriously in our daily practice. For us, rethinking pedagogy and its place in our daily life is one of the most radical actions we can take in academia, prioritizing relationship building, long-term visioning and group cohesion over strategic task-oriented planning and individual advancement.

Collegiality and collective self-management are at the core of how we work together as a team. Information sharing and transparency are fundamental principles of the relations between professors in our school. In an effort to collectivize and democratize knowledge, we share everything from syllabi to PowerPoint presentations, resources and promotion files. We assign courses against the logic of seniority, balancing individual preference and the collective needs of the department. We strive for an equitable distribution of graduate supervision as well as administrative and service work. This was designed to promote fairness, to avoid the concentration of power and information within a few individuals and to challenge the individualist principle of intellectual property. Although these structures require adjustment and continual reinforcement, the idea of its democratic basis remains.

We must also constantly re-evaluate and negotiate our educational proposals. We have created pedagogy committees of professors who are teaching to the same students that meet regularly to discuss the evolutions of the cohorts and the links they can make between their teachings. This opens a unique dialogue between and among teachers and students and allows the teacher to be situated as a member of a broader learning community. We approach the classroom as a place of prefiguration, where teaching is anchored by critical reflection on social issues and sits alongside a commitment to change and an openness to the feasibility of making it happen.

This pedagogical approach enables us to introduce theoretical texts by anchoring them in specific encounters and conversations, making them instruments through which we collectively constitute a community. We also choose to use texts that represent not only academic work but also political and activist practice, valuing these more activist texts as highly as peer-reviewed articles from colleagues. This also involves encouraging students to perceive the space they occupy and the resources they access not only from an individual perspective but as a group – and thus to collectivize their possibilities for intervention and their potential commitment to the community they find themselves in.

Putting ourselves and our students in service of the community brings life to critical thinking, allowing for the emergence of spaces of resistance and the development of dissident voices, as hooks underlines, by taking up the notion of "dissident intellectuals" or "defenders of freedom" who "are critical of the status quo and … dare to make their voices heard on behalf of justice."[32]

Questioning the dominant educational model and proposing something different comes with its challenges. For example, we crafted an undergraduate degree program primarily based on intensive courses (what we call block teaching), which brings with it a heavy administrative burden to ensure pedagogical coherence and sufficient support to students. This administrative burden was borne by us, professors, as part of our efforts to convince the university of its feasibility and relevance. The main challenge we encountered from the administration was not, interestingly, the content of our programs;[33] it was how this would impact the recruitment strategy. The main concern of our administration was whether we have enough students. The pushback over some of the more critical or radical content actually came from some of the students, who were not used to reading such texts in a university.

To support this pedagogical approach, we created a research center as well as a hybrid entity that acted as a bridge between activism and university: the Social Innovation Workshop (commonly referred to as the Atelier). The Atelier is a nonprofit organization, which, while having a certain independence from the university in terms of its governance, has an organic link with the school through their shared educational missions and close governance relationship. Concretely, it is an open workspace of some 5,000 square feet, accessible at all times, along with a lounge, meeting rooms and a collective kitchen. Members include all faculty and students in social innovation programs, as well as individuals and organizations from the community. It is a space whose goal is to support the implementation of social transformation projects. Recently, we put in place a participatory budget program to promote different initiatives proposed by the membership as well as a practice of democratic governance. The only criteria are that the activity has to be for the collective betterment of members or the wider community (that is, not for personal gain) and it has to be approved by the Atelier members.

This liminal space of convergence is a manifestation of how we think about the practice of integration in the classroom: an opportunity to work together – with members of the community – on concrete collective projects of social change. It is through these experiences that we – students, teachers, community workers – are invested together, on a daily basis, in social transformation. This process of creating a "learning community" also makes it possible for the students to become aware of the materiality of the content discussed in class, to generate shared discourses, to identify privileges, to grasp their own power to act and to discuss the potential impact of different interventions (or non-interventions) on their communities. We, as teachers, must therefore constantly negotiate our educational proposals. This is a rich process that undoubtedly improves our teaching, as it opens a unique dialogue that allows us to be situated as a member of a broad learning community. These transgressions and forms of questioning ground our relationship to the classroom and give life to our daily practice as teachers.

This tripartite structure – the school, the research center and the Atelier – allows us to build new forms of collaboration, creating a space of convergence where students can connect with organizations, activities and projects of social transformation. Thus, our pedagogy becomes a vehicle through which to promote and create social transformation within and beyond the classroom.

To radically disrupt daily university practice and refocus it on meaningful service to the community, pedagogy must be recognized as essential and fundamental to academic work. A tension is therefore evident between the teaching of critical and social justice-oriented approaches at the theoretical level and their practical implementation in academia, which refers, in our case, to the practice of professors. In our opinion, a recentering of pedagogy is one of the central elements for thinking about our daily practice, but this involves dialogue within the university community as a whole, as well as institutional support for broader processes of transformation, something that is not always evident.

Bringing an emancipatory lens to our daily practice as educators requires collective dialogue, and we need to multiply the spaces and places where we can think through these implications and explore avenues for rethinking the entire academic profession. Such a reflection can help to inform where best to apply our administrative efforts to transform our institutions. It also invites us to radically change our research and dissemination practices. At the very least, this is what happened for us within our collective process of creating new spaces.

Without presenting ourselves as a model to be replicated, we believe that similar processes – processes that acknowledge and respond to distinct realities – could be promoted in many universities if more professors took up this idea of service to the community as the core of their daily practice. Indeed, we believe that transforming our daily practice as educators is one meaningful way we can think about, and begin to create, spaces of resistance against neoliberal academic institutions. This implies reconnecting with educational aspirations and committing to teaching as a core aspect of our profession. This, of course, must be accompanied by transforming university practices, no small feat. Despite this, reconfiguring university institutions to enable strong emancipatory daily practices is at the heart of our work and our vision of social innovation.

There is a necessity, not to say an emergency, to "question the arbitrary and inauthentic fragmentation of service, teaching and research as separate categories."[34] At the Élisabeth-Bruyère School of Social Innovation, we strive for a critical and emancipatory academic praxis rooted in everyday life. The hours dedicated to teaching, research and administration can thus be articulated coherently as part of a practice anchored in the realities of the communities with whom we are in relation. Our pedagogical practice is the overarching framework that grounds our academic work in service to the community. If we are serious about the emancipatory potential of university education, we must center an engaged pedagogy as the core anchor for reimaging university.

Conclusion: Changing the scale

From impact to social transformation

Throughout this book, we have explored multiple dimensions of social innovation. Social movements, economic alternatives, collective entrepreneurship, self-management, community involvement, political action and cultural revitalization are concrete ways to meet social needs, improve the conditions of life of individuals, marginalized groups and communities and transform social relations of power. You may be asking yourself, yes, but how can you tell? Indeed, while social innovation always aims to positively impact society, this is usually difficult to measure.

Despite its popularity, we see the notion of "social impact" and its performance indicators and evaluation metrics as a slippery slope, capable of diverting social innovations away from their purpose. We are witnessing the spread of a discourse that invites community organizations and collective enterprises to direct all their efforts into growth and impact measurement rather than focusing on their social *mission* to set themselves apart from other organizations, to "demonstrate" their value with data and to attract more funding thanks to impact investment funds. A complementary discourse inspired by the world of start-ups seeks out the promising ideas from social entrepreneurs in order to inject them with a good dose of capital and coaching to *accelerate* social innovation projects; in other words, to scale-up and maximize impact. The term "impact" has become the new buzzword guiding the trajectory of social innovations from a perspective of growth and performance, paradoxically similar to the logic of the traditional private enterprise.

The Élisabeth-Bruyère School of Social Innovation approaches the question of social impact from a completely different angle. When speaking of impact, one must clarify what kind of impact is being sought. For us, social innovations should be driven by an ideal of social justice, rooted in a critical perspective attuned to systems of oppression and inspired by a thirst for emancipation, leading to a transformation of social relations and the established order. Aiming for such a broad transformation means that we cannot limit social impact to a purely quantitative dimension but need to see it as a complex and dynamic process from micro-initiatives to macrosocial change. The drivers of these types of impacts are the collective action of social movements, which resist, organize and create solidarity-based alternatives that enable local initiatives to spark sustainable structural and institutional change.

That said, social movement protest is not the only possible avenue of macrosocial change. In other periods, change was predominantly understood to be the result of technological and economic progress associated with "development" and modernization processes. This led to the classification of countries as "developed," "developing" and "underdeveloped." While this terminology is now outdated (and frankly, was problematic to begin with) and has been replaced by expressions such as "emerging countries," "Global North" and "Global South," it still reflects a vision of social change based on an evolutionist logic.

In the 1960s and 1970s, many social actors believed that this evolution could come about through a series of social and political *reforms* or, more radically, through the hope of a future *revolution*. Innovation and entrepreneurship were still far from being considered central to social change. Times change and concepts evolve: today, we must clearly define our understanding of "social transformation" and "systemic change," before they themselves become yet another buzzword devoid of real meaning.

Three forms of scaling

An influential interpretation of social change in social innovation circles involves *scaling* innovations. Scale can refer to several different things: when it is about the size or dimension of an enterprise, the volume of its business or the number of employees, growth may be the pertinent element. But a change of scale can also refer to the capacity of innovation to shift from the local to the national or even international level. Social change from this perspective is a function of the capacity of an innovation to increase its social impact by spreading and through its capacity to be exported around the world.

However, this is only one interpretation of changes of scale. Michele-Lee Moore, geographer and social innovation scholar, and Darcy J. Riddell, co-founder of Social Innovation Canada, distinguish three complementary forms of social change: scaling out, scaling up and scaling deep.[1] Scaling out attempts to increase impact through the magnitude of spread, whether through the replication or dissemination of innovation, to affect a maximum number of people and communities. Scaling up focuses on institutions, to modify laws and public policies that form the rules of the game as a way of accelerating social change. Scaling deep involves bringing about deep change through transforming cultural values and collective representations to encourage large-scale evolution in behavior, values and beliefs.

For example, social movements can expand their impact on society through techniques of mobilization that increase the numbers of individuals and groups concerned across the territory (scaling out). Then, they often target institutions to change laws, policies and access to rights, in order to dismantle the oppressive rules that reproduce structural inequalities (scaling up). Finally, they frequently adopt strategies of persuasion, framing and narrative building, which transform collective identities and established cultural values (scaling deep). Therefore, a social movement's capacity to transform society lies in a combination of these three strategies, which each reinforce and shape one another.

Social economy enterprises may seek to increase their impact by adopting strategies to improve or consolidate their services (cooperation between enterprises, diversification of services, merger-acquisition) or by replicating a successful formula: spin-offs, flexible dissemination through open innovation or social franchise, for example.[2] Collective enterprises can also decide to change the rules of the game by networking and creating alliances with social movements or working directly with governments and public institutions. Finally, they can contribute to a change in values and social representations through public outreach campaigns on a larger scale, like the Landless Workers' Movement cooperatives in Brazil, which strongly rely on base building and popular education.[3] All of these processes of changing scale can combine to increase the impact of social innovations on the world.

While there are innumerable different paths to take toward social transformation, we find that the transition from local initiative to macrosocial-level change necessarily involves some combination of these three core elements.

The four Rs to change the system

Generally, the imperative to change the "system" is rarely directly addressed in social innovation circles. Indeed, capitalism, heteropatriarchy, racism and colonialism as social systems that generate inequalities and destruction are seldom discussed or explicitly named. Sometimes, social innovation is associated with a *natural* tendency toward structural transformation, that social innovation in and of itself is somehow systemic. For example, the Réseau québécois en innovation sociale (Quebec social innovation network) provides the following definition:

> A social innovation is a new idea, approach or intervention, a new service, a new product or a new law, a new type of organization which responds more appropriately and sustainably than existing solutions to a well-defined social need, a solution that has been adopted within an institution, an organization or a community and produced a measurable benefit for the community and not just for some individuals. The significance of a social innovation is *transformative and systemic*. It constitutes, *in its inherent creativity, a break with the existing*.[4]

The idea promoted here is that social innovation will be transformative in and of itself, that its reach will be systemic from the outset and that the simple fact of being creative will be sufficient to break with the existing order. But in the view of the Élisabeth-Bruyère School of Social Innovation, if we want to change the world, we must look beyond these attractive platitudes and expressly identify and name the diverse strategies capable of transforming the structures of domination that prevail today.

One possible source of inspiration is Erik Olin Wright's book *Envisioning Real Utopias*, in which he analyzes three big strategies for social transformation: ruptural, interstitial and symbiotic transformation. The logic of rupture refers to a revolutionary perspective aimed at overthrowing the state and installing a new system of government and societal structures. Interstitial transformations, on the other hand, "seek to build new forms of social empowerment in the niches, spaces and margins of capitalist society, often where they do not seem to pose any immediate threat to dominant classes and elites."[5] Finally, symbiotic logic aims to reform institutions to remove barriers to change and foster the spread of social innovations while stabilizing the existing system.

This analytical tool helps to make strategic divergences more apparent and visible. For example, those following a logic of rupture tend to rely on confrontational strategies, while reformists, those interested in a more symbiotic transformation, attempt to access institutions to promote the scaling up of social innovations more collaboratively. Interstitial and social movement approaches, on the contrary, generally tend to develop counterpowers and operate outside institutions on the margins of established structures. Of course, these are but three categories, and it is possible to imagine many other ways of changing the system.

In his final posthumous book, Wright revised his model by outlining not just three but four strategies of social transformation: escaping, resisting, taming and dismantling the system.[6] The attempt to *escape* the existing system involves experimenting with social and solidarity innovations to increase the *resilience* of individuals, marginalized groups and communities. Here, we are in the realm of creating new systems of production, exchange and consumption to meet human needs, strengthen social cohesion and foster the capacity of societies to adapt to the potential disturbances and upheavals of economic, social, energy and ecological crises. Escape is the sphere of local initiatives, collective enterprises, self-managed groups and community involvement that aim at building a new world in the cracks of capitalism.

The strategy of *resistance*, for its part, is about struggling against various injustices or destructive projects, exercising counterpower and demanding new rights. Here, we are in the realm of social movements. *Taming* the system involves reforming institutions or collectively reappropriating them. The objective here is to use governments to promote democracy and the adoption of large-scale social measures such as basic guaranteed income, reduced work weeks, redistribution of wealth, participatory budgets, strengthened environmental regulations and so on. Taming is the world of political action, municipalism and social democracy's great advances.

Finally, *dismantling the system* refers to a democratic *rupture* and not an abrupt and authoritarian overthrow of institutions. While Wright remained skeptical about vanquishing the state and installing a new system by force, he nevertheless believed that social justice, democracy and the preservation of ecosystems require that we *go beyond* the existing system rather than just *regulate* it better. In Chapter 8, we looked at some potential avenues leading to deep democratization of economic structures, even though this remains a work in progress.

We thus have four possible strategies to change the system: resilience, resistance, reform and rupture. To better understand the differences and potential points of connection between these four Rs, we can distinguish two broad dimensions presented schematically in a table. First, we must determine whether the purpose of the strategy is to alleviate suffering, correct a situation, free up space for change or, more generally, *go beyond* the system. Next, we must define the scale of the action: is it to change the rules of the game governing the state or specific institutions or to experiment with innovations within civil society, acting within the current game? Table C.1 helps situate each approach, not to necessarily choose one strategy over the others but to clarify the different possible avenues through which to bring liberatory change to the established order.

As we have cautioned several times in this book, there isn't one single path that will necessarily lead from small-scale initiative to broad-scale social transformation. What we have sought to outline is different ingredients of emancipatory social innovation, different building blocks that, taken together, help us to better

Table C.1: The purpose of different strategies

	Alleviate suffering, free spaces	Go beyond structures
State: changing the rules of the game	Reform	Rupture
Civil society: act within the limits of the game	Resistance	Resilience

Source: Adapted from Wright, 2019, p 30

understand the structures and systems of oppression, experiment in other ways of living, organizing and building institutions and enterprises, and harness creativity and imagination to generate collective meanings and representation of future possibilities. Indeed, this last element is an important omission from this table, and from the work of Wright: the central role of education, collective identities and cultural representations, which can affect attitudes and behaviors. For this, we must look at the transformation of consciousnesses.

Reflexivity, narratives, resonance

As we said at the beginning of this book, it is important to *learn* to come together to promote collective action and the creation of democratic and effective organizations. Many of us have not yet experienced democratic forms of management or had the opportunity to participate in mass collective action. However, without a broader understanding of the societal issues and problems we seek to resolve, we risk perpetuating injustices. We must constantly reflect on society and our practices so that we can self-correct continuously and improve our functioning and our innovations. Without a good deal of individual and collective *reflexivity*, there is a real risk that dogmatism, sterile routines, inwardness and decay can consume our organizations from the inside.

Theory and practice, reflection and action, analysis of experience and living experimentation should not be placed in rigid opposition. Pedagogy and research must be central to social innovation because it is a complex and continual learning process. Collective experimentation always involves some back and forth, trial and error, successes and mistakes, sometimes leading to significant victories, sometimes to monumental failure. Instead of counting on the cult of the "positive" and success stories, it is always helpful to learn why projects fail.

For example, the Fuckup Night movement emerged out of entrepreneurial circles. Individuals share their professional failures in an honest, fun and relaxed atmosphere.[7] Fostering humility in an environment where everyone is usually trying to stand out from one another, to exchange the good and not-so-good ideas, the effective strategies and the poor decisions, helps others avoid the same mistakes. Real reflexivity must always be collective and shared, and embracing failures might be a strategy to build resilience and better projects in the future. Scaling up might not always be the best option, and sometimes the "small is beautiful" strategy might be more suitable than the "move fast and break things" motto, which is very popular among start-ups and the Silicon Valley mindset. Slowing down, taking care of communities and fostering maintenance over innovation[8] are several examples of strengthening social innovation projects and social infrastructures beyond the growth and acceleration imperative.

Another essential dimension we raised in Chapter 7 is the strategic importance of creating meaning to drive social change. Because we, as humans, live in the symbolic realm, oriented by discourses, shared beliefs and values, we must intervene in, and actively build, *collective narratives* to act on society. Whether deconstructing established discourses, (re)defining collective identities or introducing a new framing for a social question, we are involved in storytelling, naming a problem, blaming an adversary and demanding change to transform a situation.

More generally, what we are engaged in here is *reactivating* imaginaries to renew the spirit and overcome the exhaustion of utopic energies.[9] Social innovations aiming at social transformation are inspired by this *thirst for the possible*, demanding to be tested and embodied in the world.

Finally, new collective representations, narratives of emancipation and hopes for fundamental social transformation assume their full meaning when these images resonate with us. We experience resonance when a person, music or a feeling of injustice touches us, during a memorable evening with friends, or seeing a landscape, witnessing a tragedy; feeling in our bodies the vibrations of thousands of people in the streets to save the planet or collectively working on a project that has real meaning for us.

As Hartmut Rosa, sociologist and political scientist explains, resonance is not a superficial psychological state but a form of relationship to others, to oneself and to the world.[10] It arises when we are affected by something and we react to it, which generally increases our feeling of individual and collective effectiveness. When we learn how to make stuff with our own hands, decide together, start a social innovation project and resist something that will negatively affect our quality of life, we relate to the world differently. This process leaves its marks on us; it is a meaningful experience that can transform us to various degrees.

Social innovation processes are not only about meeting specific needs or transforming structures of oppression but about creating a more beautiful, convivial, democratic, responsive and humane world. The struggle against social injustice aims to ensure everyone has access to the resources and practical conditions necessary for a good and fulfilling life. Acting in a collective manner helps us to develop autonomy, to enter into resonance with others and to regain control over our conditions of existence. Experimenting, experiencing and learning are just different phases of the same process of self-transformation of reality.

The meaning of liberatory social innovation thus lies in its ability to transform the individuals bringing it forward, to make a concrete difference in lives and to provide a basis for global social change. It relies on a critical understanding of large social problems but also requires collective action and the creation of effective social organizations. All of this helps to root people in their community and to activate a capacity for engagement and collective expression of individuals and groups. Ultimately, while there must be a deep transformation of the institutions and structures of society, it is through this complex experimentation that we can expand the significance of our actions and construct the basis of a new system. Together, we can understand, judge, act, reflect, recount, resonate, innovate in the hope of changing the world.

Notes

Introduction
1. 2SLGBTQIA+ refers to Two-Spirit, Lesbian, Gay, Bisexual, Transgender, Queer, and Intersex peoples. The + is to recognize anyone who identifies as part of the gender and sexually diverse communities who may use different terminology.
2. Kinsman, 2010.
3. Luxembourg, 1905, p 22.

Chapter 1
1. Quatremère de Quincy, 1828, p 2.
2. Quatremère de Quincy, 1828, pp 11–14.
3. Godin, 2017, p 3.
4. Godin, 2017, pp 8–9.
5. Dandurand, 2005, p 378.
6. Brodie, 2018, p 8.
7. "There is no such thing as society" and "There is no alternative" are two famous pronouncements made by former British prime minister Margaret Thatcher.
8. Thomas Piketty's analysis shows that income inequality, which has increased over the last 40 years, is now as high as it was in the 19th century. See Piketty, 2013.
9. McKeen and Porter, 2003, p 125.
10. Dardot and Laval, 2009, p 5. Emphasis in original.
11. Nussbaumer and Moulaert, 2007, pp 71–88.
12. See Bouchard et al, 2016.
13. Rosa et al, 2017, pp 53–73.
14. Solé, 2008, pp 27–54; Abraham, 2016, pp 102–16.
15. Peck and Tickell, 2002, p 390.
16. Farrell, 2015, pp 254–72.
17. Economist and entrepreneur Muhammad Yunus received the Nobel Peace Prize for the invention of microcredit and the Grameen Bank (the bank of the poor) and is one of the main theorists and promoters of the social enterprise model. See Yunus, 2010.
18. Bishop and Green, 2008.
19. Laville, 2016.
20. Bélanger et al, 2007.
21. According to the Social Economy Act, adopted by Quebec in 2013.
22. Authors translation of Lévesque, 2003.
23. Arsenault, 2018, p 21.

24 Favreau and Molina, 2011.
25 Bacqué and Biewener, 2013, pp 15–16.
26 Laville, 2011.
27 Dardot and Laval, 2019. See also Harney and Moten, 2013.
28 La Pointe libertaire, 2013. Bâtiment 7 is a collectively self-managed community space offering a range of programming – including workshops, training and several social enterprises. It was founded in 2009, after a group of individuals and community organizations came together to found the nonprofit "Collectif 7 à nous" and transformed an industrial warehouse of 90,000 square feet. See https://ateliers.batiment7.org/ for further details.
29 Holloway, 2002.

Chapter 2

1 The following sections of this chapter are inspired by: Dufort, 2022, pp 12–26; Durand Folco, 2020.
2 Polyani, 2001 [1944].
3 Fraser, 2013, pp 119–32.
4 Fraser and Jaeggi, 2018.
5 Fraser, 2013.
6 Dufort, 2019.
7 Lachapelle, 2019.
8 In 2018, Nike published an ad featuring former National Football Player Colin Kaepernick, where he says, "Believe in something, even if it means sacrificing everything." Kaepernick had effectively been blacklisted from playing in the NFL after repeatedly taking a knee during the US National anthem during the 2016 season, to protest systemic discrimination against Black and racialized communities in the United States.
9 Abraham, 2018.
10 Abraham, 2016.
11 Bouchard, 2011.
12 Fligstein and McAdam, 2012.
13 Fligstein and McAdam, 2012.
14 Kluttz and Fligstein, 2016, pp 185–204.
15 Fligstein and McAdam, 2012.
16 Fligstein, 2001, pp 105–25.
17 Rosa, 2018.
18 Fligstein and McAdam, 2012.
19 Fligstein and McAdam, 2011, p 9.
20 Kluttz and Fligstein, 2016.
21 Theron, 2020.

Chapter 3

1 Macdonald, 2025.
2 Statistics Canada, 2023; CUPE, 2022; Lam, 2024.
3 Kirkup, 2016; Block and Galabuzi, 2018.

Notes

4. Office of the Correctional Investigator, 2013.
5. Office of the Correctional Investigator, 2022.
6. For more information on 2SLGBTQIA+ resources, see the Egale Canada Human Rights Trust website: https://egale.ca/resources/#category=resources
7. Tarasuk et al, 2014.
8. Reynolds, 2014, p 243.
9. Antony and Samuelson, 2017, p 6.
10. Boutilier, 2014.
11. Walker, 2023.
12. Brodie, 2018, p 11.
13. Basok and Ilcan, 2013, p 5.
14. Fraser and Honneth, 2004.
15. Fraser, 2004.
16. Pay Equity Office: Ontario, nd.
17. A statement by French President Emmanuel Macron on 3 July 2017, translated by authors. See *Le Parisien*, 2017.
18. Coulthard, 2014, p 3. See also Simpson, 2014.
19. For information about environmental racism in Nova Scotia, see The ENRICH Project: https://www.arcgis.com/home/webmap/viewer.html?webmap=d12d5f8cc46f40e5918f6072ab0e4d7c&extent=-63.6247,45.1665,-62.6105,45.5669
20. Busch, 2024.
21. Dixon and Shotwell, 2019.
22. Gibson-Graham, 2006, p xxiii.
23. Gibson-Graham et al, 2006, p 11.
24. Cited in the prologue to Manier, 2012.
25. Haiven and Khasnabish, 2010.
26. Latouche, 2011.
27. Siltanen et al, 2014, pp 1–20.
28. The notion of "real utopias" is discussed in greater detail in Chapter 8.
29. Wright, 2010.
30. Davis, 2016.

Chapter 4

1. Al-Saji, 2020, p 102.
2. Kosofsky Sedgwick, 2003, p 139.
3. Sedgwick, 2003, p 146.
4. Alfred, 1995, p 8.
5. Alfred, 2009, p 34.
6. Alfred, 2009, p 24.
7. Alfred, 2009, p 25.
8. Alfred, 2009, p 60.
9. Alfred, 2009, pp 24–5.
10. Simpson, 2014, p 28.
11. Palmater, 2019.
12. Alfred, 2009, p 27.

13. Alfred, 2009, p 34.
14. Alfred, 2009, p 35.
15. Hardt, 2023, p 2.
16. Azoulay, 2019, p 44.
17. Muñoz, 2009, p 9.
18. Cabral, 1979, p 128.
19. Cabral, 1979, p 130.
20. Cabral, 1979, p 134.
21. Cabral, 1979, p 132.
22. Cabral, 1979, p 133.
23. Bloch, 1986, p 227.
24. Bloch, 1986, p 235.
25. Philip, 2008, p 189.
26. Hartman, 2008, p 11.
27. Hartman, 2008, p 11.

Chapter 5

1. Suyemoto et al, 2022, p 37.
2. Collins and Bilge, 2020, p 52.
3. Cho et al, 2013, p 795.
4. Combahee River Collective, 1977.
5. Crenshaw, 1989.
6. Collins and Bilge, 2020.
7. National Inquiry into Missing and Murdered Indigenous Women and Girls, 2019.
8. Burczycka and Cotter, 2023, pp 1–34.
9. Hankivsky and Mussell, 2018, p 304.
10. Evans and Lépinard, 2020, p 5.
11. Evans and Lépinard, 2020, p 5.
12. Tuck and Yang, 2012, pp 1–40.
13. Palmater, 2019.
14. Simpson, 2011, p 16.
15. Simpson, 2011, p 17.
16. Ahmed, 2012.
17. brown, 2020, p 40.
18. brown, 2020, p 40.
19. brown, 2020, p 8.

Chapter 6

1. Morales Hudon and Sarrasin, 2019, pp 99–118.
2. Olson, 2011.
3. Gurr, 2012.
4. Translation by authors. Neveu, 2011, p 43.
5. Oberschall, 1973.
6. For more on this movement, see McAdam, 1999.
7. Tilly, 1976, p 143.
8. See, for example: Goodhand, 2017.

9. See, for example: Loreto, 2020.
10. Tiny homes are compact living structures, often the size of sheds or trailers, containing basic housing elements. They have primarily emerged in North America as a response to homelessness and housing affordability, and for those seeking a more off-grid or secluded existence.
11. Tufekci, 2020.

Chapter 7
1. Felstiner et al, 1991, pp 41–54.
2. Neveu, 2011, p 77.
3. Goffman, 1986.
4. Benford and Snow, 2000, pp 611–39.
5. Benford and Snow, 2000, p 619.
6. Benford and Snow, 2000, p 619.
7. Among the best known are: Ewen, 2001 [1976]; Stauber and Rampton, 2002 [1995].
8. Levine, 1994; for more information on the Yes Men, see https://theyesmen.org
9. Translation by authors. Gagnon, 2017.
10. Gagnon, 2017.
11. Morales Hudon and Sarrasin, 2019, p 102.
12. The Truth and Reconciliation Commission of Canada, 2015.

Chapter 8
1. For more on the dynamic of value accumulation, see Postone, 1993.
2. For more on the dynamic of the acceleration of technological development, sociocultural change and rhythm, see Rosa, 2010.
3. Fraser, 2014, pp 55–72.
4. On this topic, see Bourgault and Perreault, 2015.
5. Fraser, 2014, p 71.
6. Robert and Toupin, 2018.
7. Robert and Toupin, 2018, p 10.
8. Laville, 2013.
9. Gorz, 1999.
10. Cukier, 2023.
11. Here we are critiquing the model proposed by Mintzberg, 2016.
12. Devine, 1988; Elson, 1988; Albert and Hahnel, 1991; Cockshott and Cottrell, 1993; Bookchin, 2005; Wright, 2010.
13. Dardot and Laval, 2019, p 1.
14. Ostrom, 1990.
15. See, for example, the Madison Area Community Land Trust in Madison: https://affordablehome.org/
16. For a rich portrait of the commons, see Bollier and Helfrich, 2019.
17. See Durand Folco, 2017.
18. Bauwens et al, 2019.
19. Latouche, 2018, pp 277–84; Hickel, 2020.
20. Abraham, 2019.

21. Rosa, 2018, p 503.
22. Robra et al, 2020; Dengler and Lang, 2022, pp 1–28; Latouche, 2024, pp 155–66.
23. Saito, 2024, p 126.
24. Wright, 2010, p 12.

Chapter 9

1. Carland et al, 1984, pp 354–9.
2. For a more detailed study of the field of entrepreneurship, see Filion, 1997, pp 129–71.
3. Fontan, 2011, p 39.
4. Say, 1972 [1803], p 66.
5. Schumpeter, 1942.
6. Fontan, 2011, p 40.
7. Geissinger et al, 2020, p 8.
8. Schumpeter, 1942.
9. Innovation, Science and Economic Development Canada, 2023.
10. Robichaud and Turmel, 2012.
11. Harper, 2008, pp 613–26; De Mol et al, 2015, pp 232–55.
12. Translation by authors. Fontan, 2011, p 43.
13. See https://theindexproject.org/award/nominees/2015. Unfortunately Bibak is no longer in operation.
14. The examples in this chapter originate from Stambouli, 2021, pp 155–8.
15. Cook and Plunkett, 2006, pp 421–8.
16. Cook and Plunkett, 2006, p 35.
17. Dash, 2014, pp 6–29.
18. International Cooperative Alliance, 2023.
19. For more information, see the Ontario Co-operative Association website: https://ontario.coop/co-operative-principles
20. Romeo, 2022.
21. Mondragon, nd.
22. For more information about these funding tools, see Bellemare et al, 2017.
23. Hughes, 2013.
24. Nova Scotia Securities Commission, nd.
25. For more about Thèsez-vous, see https://www.thesez-vous.com/
26. Social Innovation and Social Finance Strategy Co-Creation Steering Group, 2018, p 17.
27. For more about these risks, see the work of TIESS (Territoires innovants en économie sociale et solidaire): https://tiess.ca/outils/12-les-impacts-negatifs-potentiels-de-la-mesure-dimpact
28. Montreal Declaration on evaluation and social impact measurement, 2019.

Chapter 10

1. Bourdet and Gillerm, 1975.
2. For more on these organizational models, see Peters, 1993; Laloux, 2014; Getz, 2017.

3. Boltanski and Chiapello, 1999.
4. Gilligan, 2008.
5. Delassus, 2015.
6. Shang and Chandra, 2017.
7. Graeber, 2013.
8. Kropotkine, 2001.
9. Collective Work, 2017.
10. Bolloten, 2014.
11. Rosanvallon, 1976.
12. See https://librairieleuguelionne.com; https://coopcycle.org/fr
13. For more information, see the 2009 documentary film *Marinaleda, un village en utopie* by Sophie Bolze.
14. Quijoux, 2011, pp 91–105.
15. Chambat, 2015.
16. Christian, 2015.
17. For more, see Cukier, 2018, pp 190–2.
18. See www.recuperadasdoc.com.ar
19. Charest, 2007.
20. Withers, 2012.
21. Vercauteren, 2011.

Chapter 11
1. Favreau, 1989.
2. Talpin, 2016.
3. Freire, 1974.
4. Alinsky, 1989, p xix.
5. Bacqué and Biewener, 2013.
6. Alinsky, 1989.
7. For a more comprehensive guide on tools and techniques of intervention, see Lavoie and Panet-Raymond, 2014.
8. Cited in Zamora and Görtz, 2014.
9. Sintomer, 2007.
10. Bacqué et al, 2005, p 11.
11. Blondiaux, 2008.
12. Maillé and Batellier, 2017.
13. Arnstein, 1969, pp 216–24.
14. For a detailed analysis of democratic deliberation, see Le Goff and Girard, 2010.
15. Landemore, 2013.
16. Bonin, 2017.
17. Lewis and Slitine, 2016.
18. Sintomer et al, 2014.
19. Baiocchi, 2003, pp 45–76.
20. For a practical manual explaining the workings of a participatory budget, see Rabouin, 2009; for a look at participatory budget experiences in Quebec, see www.budgetparticipatifquebec.ca/fr

[21] The neologism "asphaltiste" was coined by Gatineau municipal councillor Mike Duggan, who used it for the first time in May 2017.
[22] Béïque, 2011.
[23] For a detailed study of Guyenne's cooperative model, see Laplante, 1994; for a more fun, comic strip presentation, see Desharnais, 2018.
[24] Durand Folco, 2017.
[25] For a pedagogical overview of Bookchin's thought, see Biehl, 2013.
[26] For a detailed account of these three municipal waves, see Lamant, 2016; Akuno and Nangwaya, 2017; Grojean, 2017.

Chapter 12
[1] Bourdieu and Darbel, 1990 [1986].
[2] Williams, 1959, p 114.
[3] Gibson, 2008, pp 247–57.
[4] Bennett, 1995; Bennett, 2003, pp 180–8.
[5] Malraux, 2002 [1966], pp 55–61.
[6] Pelletier, 1972, pp 219–22.
[7] The Truth and Reconciliation Commission of Canada refers to residential schools as a central part of the cultural genocide enacted against Indigenous Peoples.
[8] Union of Ontario Indians, 2013, p 3.
[9] Bennett, 2007, pp 610–29.
[10] Bennett, 1992, pp 395–408.
[11] Belfiore, 2002, pp 37–41.
[12] International Council of Museums, 1971.
[13] Desrosiers and Lafleur, 1981.
[14] L'Écomusée du fier monde, 2016.
[15] Binette, 2009, pp 129–50.
[16] Dean and Keys, 2015.
[17] Daveluy and Coupal, 2016.
[18] Écomusée du patrimoine funéraire et commémoratif, nd.
[19] Hooper-Greenhill, 1992; Bennett, 1995, 2004.
[20] Isar, 1985, p 184.
[21] Rivière, 1985, pp 182–3.
[22] Écomusée du patrimoine funéraire et commémoratif, 2023.
[23] Écomusée du patrimoine funéraire et commémoratif, 2021.
[24] Écomusée du patrimoine funéraire et commémoratif, 2021.
[25] Tremblay, 2022.

Chapter 13
[1] This chapter draws on Dufort and Morales Hudon, 2020.
[2] hooks, 1994.
[3] hooks, 1994, p 205.
[4] hooks, 2003, p 83.
[5] Brownlee, 2016, pp 17–21.
[6] Webber and Butovsky, 2018, pp 165–81.

Notes

7. Webber and Butovsky, 2018.
8. Schimanski and Alperin, 2018, pp 1–21.
9. Schimanski and Alperin, 2018.
10. Brownlee, 2016; Webber and Butovsky, 2018.
11. Acker and Webber, 2016, pp 233–55.
12. Fontan et al, 2018, pp 195–224.
13. For criticism of the university as alienating, see Berg and Seeber, 2016; for criticism of how the university is exclusive, see Ahmed, 2012; Frances et al, 2017, pp 300–14.
14. Calhoun, 2008, pp xiii–xxvi.
15. Fontan et al, 2018, p 196.
16. Berg and Seeber, 2016.
17. Brownlee, 2016.
18. Clark et al, 2009.
19. hooks, 2003, p 83.
20. Freire, 1967.
21. Schimaki and Alpera, 2018.
22. Freire, 1998, p 30.
23. González-Monteagudo, 2002, pp 49–65.
24. González-Monteagudo, 2002, p 91.
25. Mohanty, 1989, pp 179–208.
26. hooks, 1994, p 147.
27. hooks, 1994, p 12.
28. hooks, 1994, p 2.
29. hooks, 1994, p 139.
30. hooks, 1994, p 34.
31. hooks, 1994, p 12.
32. hooks, 2003, p 187.
33. The content of our BA is unique in that it includes two mandatory courses on issues of antiracism, two mandatory courses on feminist perspectives and a mandatory course on capitalism, class and worker movements.
34. Kiang, 2008.

Conclusion

1. Moore and Riddell, 2015.
2. For a more comprehensive overview, see the practical guide, Bellemare et al, 2017.
3. Hevia-Pacheco and Vergara-Camus, 2010.
4. Emphasis added. Réseau québécois en innovation sociale, 2011.
5. Wright, 2010, p 305.
6. See Wright, 2019.
7. For more, visit Fuckup Night's website: https://fuckupnights.com
8. Russell and Vinsel, 2016.
9. Habermas, 1990, pp 103–26.
10. Rosa, 2018.

References

Abraham, Y.-M. (2016) 'L'innovation sociale comme champ!', course notes, week three, MNGT 60424, Concevoir et gérer l'innovation sociale, HEC Montréal.

Abraham, Y.-M. (2018) 'À quoi sert l'innovation sociale?', paper presented at The Great Transition Conference, Montreal, May.

Abraham, Y.-M. (2019) *Guérir du mal de l'infini: produire moins, partager plus, décider ensemble*, Montreal: Écosociété.

Acker, S. and Webber, M. (2016) 'Discipline and Publish: The Tenure Review Process in Ontario Universities', in L. Shultz and M. Viczko (eds) *Assembling and Governing the Higher Education Institution*, London: Palgrave Macmillan, pp 233–55.

Ahmed, S. (2012) *On Being Included: Racism and Diversity in Institutional Life*, Durham, NC: Duke University Press.

Akuno, K. and Nangwaya, A. (eds) (2017) *Jackson Rising: The Struggle for Economic Democracy and Black Self-Determination in Jackson*, Montreal: Daraja Press.

Albert, M. and Hahnel, R. (1991) *The Political Economy of Participatory Economics*, Princeton, NJ: Princeton University Press.

Alfred, G.R. (1995) *Heeding the Voices of Our Ancestors: Kahnawake Mohawk Politics and the Rise of Native Nationalism*, Toronto: Oxford University Press.

Alfred, T. (2009) *Wasáse: Indigenous Pathways of Action and Freedom*, Toronto: University of Toronto Press.

Alinsky, S. (1989) *Rules for Radicals: A Practical Primer for Realistic Radicals*, New York: Vintage Books.

Al-Saji, A. (2020) 'Durée', in G. Lewis, A.V. Murphy and G. Salamon (eds) *50 Concepts for a Critical Phenomenology*, Evanston: Northwestern University Press, pp 99–106.

Antony, W. and Samuelson, L. (2017) *Power and Resistance: Critical Thinking about Canadian Social Issues*, Winnipeg, MB: Fernwood Publishing.

References

Arnstein, S. (1969) 'A Ladder of Citizen Participation', *Journal of the American Institute of Planners*, 35(4): 216–24.

Arsenault, G. (2018) *L'économie sociale au Québec: une perspective politique*, Quebec: Presse de l'Université du Québec.

Azoulay, A.A. (2019) *Potential History: Unlearning Imperialism*, London: Verso.

Bacqué, M.-H. and Biewener, C. (2013) *L'empowerment: une pratique émancipatrice?*, Paris: La Découverte.

Bacqué, M.-H., Rey, H. and Sintomer, Y. (2005) 'La démocratie participative, un nouveau paradigme de l'action publique?', in M.-H. Bacqué, H. Rey and Y. Sintomer (eds) *Gestion de proximité et démocratie participative: une perspective comparative*, Paris: La Découverte, pp 9–46.

Baiocchi, G. (2003) 'Participation, Activism, and Politics: The Porto Alegre Experiment', in A. Fung and E.O. Wright (eds) *Deepening Democracy: Institutional Innovations in Empowered Participatory Governance*, New York: Verso, pp 45–76.

Basok, T. and Ilcan, S. (2013) *Issues in Social Justice: Citizenship and Transnational Struggles*, Oxford: Oxford University Press.

Bauwens, M., Kostakis, V. and Pazaitis, A. (2019) *Peer to Peer: The Commons Manifesto*, London: University of Westminster Press.

Béïque, J. (2011) *Saint-Camille: le pari de la convivialité*, Montreal: Écosociété.

Bélanger, P.R., Boucher, J. and Lévesque, B. (2007) 'L'économie solidaire en Amérique du Nord: le cas du Québec', in J.-L. Laville (ed) *L'économie solidaire: une perspective internationale*, Paris: Hachette Littératures, pp 106–43.

Belfiore, E. (2002) 'Art as a Means of Alleviating Social Exclusion: Does It Really Work? A Critique of Instrumental Cultural Policies and Social Impact Studies in the UK', *International Journal of Cultural Policy*, 8(1): 37–41.

Bellemare, M.-F., Léonard, M. and Lagacé-Brunet, P. (2017) 'Changer d'échelle en économie sociale: planifier l'essor et décupler les retombées de votre entreprise d'économie sociale', Montreal: Territoires innovants en économie sociale et solidaire (TIESS).

Benford, R.D. and Snow, D.A. (2000) 'Framing Processes and Social Movements: An Overview and Assessment', *Annual Review of Sociology*, 26: 611–39.

Bennett, T. (1992) 'Useful Culture', *Cultural Studies*, 6(3): 395–408.

Bennett, T. (1995) *The Birth of the Museum: History, Theory, Politics*, London: Routledge.

Bennett, T. (2003) 'The Political Rationality of the Museum', in J. Lewis and T. Miller (eds) *Critical Cultural Policy Studies: A Reader*, Oxford: Blackwell Publishing, pp 180–8.

Bennett, T. (2004) *Pasts Beyond Memory Evolution, Museums, Colonialism*, London: Routledge.

Bennett, T. (2007) 'Making Culture, Changing Society', *Cultural Studies*, 21(4–5): 610–29.

Berg, M. and Seeber, B.K. (2016) *The Slow Professor: Challenging the Culture of Speed in the Academy*, Toronto: University of Toronto Press.

Biehl, J. (2013) *Le municipalisme libertaire: la politique de l'écologie sociale*, Montreal: Écosociété.

Binette, R. (2009) 'La contribution des institutions muséales au "capital social": cas de l'Écomusée du fier monde (Montréal, Canada)', in I.A. Urtizberea (ed) *Activaciones patrimoniales e iniciativas museisticas: ¿Por quién? y ¿Para qué?*, Barrio Sarriena: Servicio Editorial de la Universidad del País Vasco, pp 129–50.

Bishop, M. and Green, M. (2008) *Philanthrocapitalism: How the Rich Can Save The World, and Why We Should Let Them*, London: Bloomsbury Press.

Bloch, E. (1986) *The Principle of Hope*, Cambridge, MA: MIT Press.

Block, S. and Galabuzi, G.-E. (2018) 'Persistent Inequality: Ontario's Colour-Coded Labour Market', Ontario: Canadian Centre for Policy Alternatives.

Blondiaux, L. (2008) *Le nouvel esprit de la démocratie: actualité de la démocratie participative*, Paris: Seuil.

Bollier, D. and Helfrich, S. (2019) *Free, Fair and Alive: The Insurgent Power of the Commons*, Gabriola Island: New Society Publishers.

Bolloten, B. (2014) *La guerre d'Espagne: révolution et contrerévolution (1934–1939)*, Paris: Agone.

Boltanski, L. and Chiapello, È. (1999) *Le nouvel esprit du capitalisme*, Paris: Gallimard.

Bolze, S. (2009) *Marinaleda, un village en utopie* [DVCAM], Tarmak Films.

Bonin, H. (2017) *La démocratie hasardeuse: essai sur le tirage au sort en politique*, Montreal: XYZ.

References

Bookchin, M. (2005) *The Ecology of Freedom*, Oakland: AK Press.

Bouchard, M.J. (ed) (2011) *L'économie sociale vecteur d'innovation: l'expérience du Québec*, Quebec: University of Quebec Press.

Bourdet, Y. and Guillerm, A. (1975) *Clefs pour l'autogestion*, Paris: Seghers.

Bourdieu, P. and Darbel, A. (1990 [1986]) *The Love of Art*, Stanford: Stanford University Press.

Bourgault, S. and Perreault, J. (eds) (2015) *Le care: éthique féministe actuelle*, Montreal: Remue-ménage.

Boutilier, A. (2014) 'Native Teen's Slaying a "Crime," Not a "Sociological Phenomenon," Stephen Harper Says', *Toronto Star*, 21 August.

Brodie, J. (2018) *Contemporary Inequalities and Social Justice in Canada*, Toronto: University of Toronto Press.

brown, a.m. (2020) *We Will Not Cancel Us: And Other Dreams of Transformative Justice*, Chico, CA: AK Press.

Brownlee, J. (2016) 'The Role of Governments in Corporatizing Canadian Universities', *Academic Matters*, January: 17–21.

Burczycka, M. and Cotter, A. (2023) 'Court Outcomes in Homicides of Indigenous Women and Girls, 2009 to 2021', Juristat, pp 1–34.

Busch, J. (2024) 'Climate Change and Development in Three Charts: An Update', Centre for Global Development, Available from: https://www.cgdev.org/blog/climate-and-development-three-charts-update

Cabral, A. (1979) *Unity and Struggle: Speeches and Writings of Amilcar*, New York: Monthly Review Press.

Calhoun, C. (2008) 'Foreword', in C.R. Hale (ed) *Engaging Contradictions: Theory, Politics, and Methods of Activist Scholarship*, Berkeley: University of California Press, pp xiii–xxvi.

Canadian Research Institute for the Advancement of Women (2021) 'Feminist intersectionality', Ottawa, ON: CRIAW, Available from: www.criaw-icref.ca/publications/feminist-intersectionality-primer/

Carland, J., Hoy, F., Boulton, W.R. and Carland, J.A.C. (1984) 'Differentiating Entrepreneurs from Small Business Owners: A Conceptualization', *The Academy of Management Review*, 9(2): 354–9.

Center for Story-based Strategy and Interaction Institute for Social Change (nd) '#The4thBox', Available from: https://www.storybasedstrategy.org/the4thbox

Chambat, G. (2015) *Pédagogie et révolution: questions de classe et (re)lectures pédagogiques*, Paris: Libertalia.

Charest, G. (2007) *La démocratie se meurt: vive la sociocratie!*, Paris: Esserci.

Cho, S., Crenshaw, K.W. and McCall, L. (2013) 'Toward a Field of Intersectionality Studies: Theory, Applications, and Praxis', *Signs: Journal of Women in Culture and Society*, 38(4): 785–810.

Christian, D.L. (2015) *Vivre autrement: écovillages, communautés et cohabitats*, Montreal: Écosociété.

Clark, I.D., Moran, G., Skolnik, M.L. and Trick, D. (2009) *Academic Transformation: The Forces Reshaping Higher Education in Ontario*, Queen's Policy Studies Series, Montreal: McGill–Queen's University Press.

Cockshott, P. and Cottrell, A. (1993) *Towards a New Socialism*, Nottingham: Spokesman.

Collective Work (2017) *De l'autogestion: théorie et pratique*, Paris: Éditions CNT.

Collins, P.H. and Bilge, S. (2020) *Intersectionality*, Cambridge: Polity.

Combahee River Collective (1977) *The Combahee River Collective Statement*, Seattle: Black Past.

Cook, M. and Plunkett, B. (2006) 'Collective Entrepreneurship: An Emerging Phenomenon in Producer-Owned Organizations', *Journal of Agricultural and Applied Economics*, 38(2): 421–8.

Coulthard, G. (2014) *Red Skin, White Masks: Rejecting the Colonial Politics of Recognition*, Minneapolis: Minnesota University Press.

Crenshaw, K. (1989) 'Demarginalizing the Intersection of Race and Sex: A Black Feminist Critique of Antidiscrimination Doctrine, Feminist Theory and Antiracist Politics', *University of Chicago Legal Forum*, 1: 139–67.

Cukier, A. (2018) *Le travail démocratique*, Paris: Presses Universitaires de France.

Cukier, A. (2023) *Democratic Work: Radical Democracy and the Future of Labour*, Cham: Palgrave Macmillan.

References

CUPE [Canadian Union of Public Employees] (2022) 'Wage growth vs. Inflation', *Economy at Work*, Spring, Available from: https://cupe.ca/sites/cupe/files/field_publication_past_issues/economy_at_work_spring_2022_e_fnl.pdf

Dandurand, L. (2005) 'Réflexion autour du concept d'innovation sociale, approche historique et comparative', *Revue française d'administration publique*, 3(115): 377–88.

Dardot, P. and Laval, C. (2009) *La nouvelle raison du monde: essai sur la société néolibérale*, Paris: La Découverte.

Dardot, P. and Laval, C. (2019) *Common: On Revolution in the 21st Century*, London: Bloomsbury Publishing.

Dash, A. (2014) 'Toward an Epistemological Foundation for Social and Solidarity Economy', United Nations Research Institute for Social Development Occasional Paper: Potential and Limits of Social and Solidarity Economy, 3.

Daveluy, P. and Coupal, E. (2016) 'Les cimetières de la ville', Encyclopédie du MEM, Available from: https://ville.montreal.qc.ca/memoiresdesmontrealais/les-cimetieres-de-la-ville

Davis, A. (2016) *Freedom Is a Constant Struggle: Ferguson, Palestine, and the Foundations of a Movement*, Chicago: Haymarket Books.

Dean, D. (2015) 'Alternative Histories of Work and Labour in the National Capital Region', paper presented at Active History Conference, Huron University College, 3 October.

Delassus, E. (2015) 'Manager selon le care', *Qualitique* [Preprint], (266).

De Mol, E., Khapova, S.N. and Elfring, T. (2015) 'Entrepreneurial Team Cognition: A Review', *International Journal of Management Reviews*, 17(6): 232–55.

Dengler, C. and Lang, M. (2022) 'Commoning Care: Feminist Degrowth Visions for a Socio-Ecological Transformation', *Feminist Economics*, 28(1): 1–28.

Desharnais, F. (2018) *La petite Russie*, Montreal: Pow Pow.

Desrosiers, G. and Lafleur, G. (1981) *La Maison du fier monde*, Montreal: La maison du fier monde.

Devine, P. (1988) *Democracy and Economic Planning: The Political Economy of a Self-Governing Society*, Boulder: Westview Press.

Dixon, C. and Shotwell, A. (2019) 'For a Grieving Optimism', *Canadian Dimension*, 52(3).

Dufort, P. (2019) 'L'innovation sociale émancipatrice: fondements théoriques néopolanyiens', Centre de recherche sur les innovations et les transformations sociales, 1, Available from: https://innovationsocialeusp.ca/wp-content/uploads/2019/12/Note-1-Dufort-IS-e%CC%81mancipatrice-1.pdf

Dufort, P. (2022) 'L'innovation sociale émancipatrice: fondements théoriques néopolanyiens', *Canadian Journal of Nonprofit and Social Economy Research*, 13(1): 12–26.

Dufort, P. and Morales Hudon, A. (2020) 'N'étions nous pas des enseignant.e.s? Décentrer notre pratique universitaire de la recherche', *Revue Possibles*, 44(2): 69–78.

Durand Folco, J. (2017) *À nous la ville! Traité du municipalisme*, Montreal: Écosociété.

Durand Folco, J. (2020) 'L'innovation sociale comme champ de bataille', Centre de recherche sur les innovations et les transformations sociales, Carnets du CRITS, Available from: https://innovationsocialeusp.ca/crits/blogue/linnovation-sociale-comme-champ-de-bataille

L'Écomusée du fier monde (2006) 'À cœur de jour! Grandeurs et misères d'un quartier populaire', Available from: https://ecomusee.qc.ca/evenement/a-coeur-de-jour-grandeurs-et-miseres-dun-quartier-populaire/

Écomusée du patrimoine funéraire et commémoratif (nd) 'À propos de l'Écomusée', Available from: https://ecomuseedupatrimoine.org/a-propos/

Écomusée du patrimoine funéraire et commémoratif (2021) 'Notre modèle thématique', Available from: https://ecomuseedupatrimoine.org/a-propos/notre-modele-thematique/

Écomusée du patrimoine funéraire et commémoratif (2023) 'Alain Tremblay', Available from: https://ecomuseedupatrimoine.org/author/alain-tremblay/

Elson, D. (1988) 'Market Socialism or Socialization of the Market?', *New Left Review*, 172: 3–44.

Evans, E. and Lépinard, É. (eds) (2020) *Intersectionality in Feminist and Queer Movements: Confronting Privileges*, London: Routledge.

Ewen, S. (2001) *Captains of Consciousness: Advertising and the Social Roots of the Consumer Culture*, New York: Basic Books.

Farrell, N. (2015) '"Conscience Capitalism" and the Neoliberalisation of the Non-Profit Sector', *New Political Economy*, 20(2): 254–72.

Favreau, L. (1989) *Mouvement populaire et intervention communautaire de 1960 à nos jours: continuités et ruptures*, Montreal: Le Centre de formation populaire/Éditions du Fleuve.

Favreau, L. and Molina, E. (2011) *Économie et société: pistes pour une sortie de crise*, Montreal: Presses de l'Université du Québec.

Felstiner, W., Abel, R. and Sarat, A. (1991) 'L'émergence et la transformation des litiges: réaliser, reprocher et réclamer', *Politix*, 16: 41–54.

Filion, L.J. (1997) 'Le champ de l'entrepreneuriat: historique, évolution, tendances', *Revue internationale PME*, 10(2): 129–71.

Fligstein, N. (2001) 'Social Skill and the Theory of Fields', *Sociological Theory*, 19(2): 105–25.

Fligstein, N. and McAdam, D. (2011) 'Toward a General Theory of Strategic Action Fields', *Sociological Theory*, 29(1): 1–26.

Fligstein, N. and McAdam, D. (2012) *A Theory of Fields*, Oxford: Oxford University Press.

Fontan, J.-M. (2011) 'Entreprenariat social et entreprenariat collectif: synthèse et constats', *Revue canadienne de recherche sur les OBSL et l'économie sociale*, 2(2): 37–56.

Fontan, J.-M., Alberio, M., Belley, S., Chiasson, G., Houssine, D., Lafranchise, N. et al (2018) 'Activités de "recherche avec" au sein du réseau de l'Université du Québec', *Recherches sociographiques*, 59(1–2): 195–224.

Frances, H., Dua, E., Kobayashi, A., James, C., Li, P., Ramos, H. et al (2017) 'Race, Racialization and Indigeneity in Canadian Universities', *Race Ethnicity and Education*, 20(3): 300–14.

Fraser, N. (2013) 'A Triple Movement?', *New Left Review*, 81: 119–32.

Fraser, N. (2014) 'Behind Marx's Hidden Abode', *New Left Review*, 86: 55–72.

Fraser, N. and Honneth, A. (2004) *Redistribution or Recognition? A Political–Philosophical Exchange*, New York: Verso.

Fraser, N. and Jaeggi, R. (2018) *Capitalism: A Conversation in Critical Theory*, New York: Verso.

Freire, P. (1967) *L'éducation comme pratique de la liberté*, Paris: Édition du Cerf.

Freire, P. (1974) *Pédagogie des opprimés*, Paris: Maspero.

Freire, P. (1998) *Pedagogy of Freedom*, Lanham: Roman & Littlefield.

Froehle, C. (2016) 'The Evolution of an Accidental Meme', Medium.

Gagnon, M.-A. (2017) 'SOS Montfort', L'Encyclopédie canadienne, Available from https://www.thecanadianencyclopedia.ca/fr/article/sos-montfort

Geissinger, A., Laurell, C. and Sandström, C. (2020) 'Digital Disruption beyond Uber and Airbnb: Tracking the Long Tail of the Sharing Economy', *Technological Forecasting and Social Change*, 155: 119323.

Getz, I. (2017) *L'entreprise libérée: comment devenir un leader libérateur et se désintoxiquer des vieux modèles*, Paris: Fayard.

Gibson, L. (2008) 'In Defence of Instrumentality', *Cultural Trends*, 17(4): 247–57.

Gibson-Graham, J.K. (2006) *A Postcapitalist Politics*, Minneapolis: University of Minnesota Press.

Gibson-Graham, J.K., Cameron, J. and Healy, S. (2006) *Take Back the Economy: An Ethical Guide for Transforming Our Communities*, Minneapolis: University of Minnesota Press.

Gilligan, C. (2008) *Une voix différente: pour une éthique du care*, Paris: Flammarion.

Godin, B. (2017) *L'innovation sous tension: histoire d'un concept*, Quebec: Laval University Press.

Goffman, E. (1986) *Frame Analysis: An Essay on the Organization of the Experience*, Boston: Northeastern University Press.

González-Monteagudo, J. (2002) 'Les pédagogies critiques chez Paulo Freire et leur audience actuelle', *Pratiques de Formation/Analyses*, 43: 49–65.

Goodhand, M. (2017) *Runaway Wives and Rogue Feminists. The Origins of the Women's Shelter Movement in Canada*, Halifax: Fernwood Publishing.

Gorz, A. (1999) *Reclaiming Work: Beyond the Wage-Based Society*, Cambridge: Polity.

Graeber, D. (2013) *The Democracy Project: A History, a Crisis, a Movement*, New York: Random House.

Grojean, O. (2017) *La révolution kurde: le PKK et la fabrique d'une utopie*, Paris: La Découverte.

Gurr, T.R. (2012) *Why Men Rebel*, London: Routledge.

Habermas, J. (1990) 'La crise de l'État-providence et l'épuisement des énergies utopiques', in *Écrits politiques*, Paris: Le Cerf, pp 103–26.

References

Haiven, M. and Khasnabish, A. (2010) 'What Is Radical Imagination?', *Affinities*, 4(2): i–xxxvii.

Hankivsky, O. and Mussell, L. (2018) 'Gender-Based Analysis Plus in Canada: Problems and Possibilities of Integrating Intersectionality', *Canadian Public Policy*, 44(4): 303–16.

Hardt, M. (2023) *The Subversive Seventies*, Oxford: Oxford University Press.

Harney, S. and Moten, F. (2013) *The Undercommons: Fugitive Planning and Black Study*, New York: Minor Compositions.

Harper, D. (2008) 'Towards a theory of entrepreneurial teams', *Journal of Business Venturing*, 23(6): 613–26.

Hartman, S. (2008) 'Venus in Two Acts', *Small Axe*, 12(2): 1–14.

Hevia-Pacheco, P. and Vergara-Camus, L. (2010) 'Éducation populaire et émancipation: l'expérience des travailleurs ruraux sans terre au Brésil', *Éducation Canada*, 45(3): 11–15.

Hickel, J. (2020) *Less Is More: How Degrowth Will Save the World*, New York: Penguin Random House.

Holloway, J. (2002) *Change the World without Taking Power: The Meaning of Revolution Today*, London: Pluto Press.

hooks, b. (1994) *Teaching to Transgress: Education as the Practice of Freedom*, New York: Routledge.

hooks, b. (2003) *Teaching Community: A Pedagogy of Hope*, New York: Routledge.

Hooper Greenhill, E. (1992) *Museums and the Shaping of Knowledge*, London: Routledge.

Hughes, S. (2013) 'Community Bonds: A Non-Profit Financing Tool', Vancouver: Vancity Community Foundation.

Innovation, Science and Economic Development Canada (2023) 'Key Small Business Statistics 2023', Ottawa: Government of Canada, Available from: https://ised-isde.canada.ca/site/sme-research-statistics/sites/default/files/documents/2023-ksbs-en.pdf

International Cooperative Alliance (2023) 'Cooperatives Are Building a Better World: Discover How!', Available from: https://ica.coop/

International Council of Museums (1971) 'General Assembly: The Museum in the Service of Man; Resolution 1', Grenoble, France, 10 September.

Isar, Y.R. (1985) 'Editorial for Images of the Ecomuseum', *Museum International*, 37(4): 184.

Kiang, P.N. (2008) 'Crouching Activists, Hidden Scholars: Reflections on Research and Development with Students and Communities in Asian American Studies', in C.R. Hale (ed) *Engaging Contradictions: Theory, Politics, and Methods of Activist Scholarship*, Berkeley: University of California Press, pp 299–318.

Kinsman, G. (2010) 'Queer Liberation: The Social Organization of Forgetting and the Resistance of Remembering', Canadian Dimension, Available from: https://canadiandimension.com/articles/view/queer-liberation-the-social-organization-of-forgetting-and-the-resistance-o

Kirkup, K. (2016) 'Liberal Budget Includes Billions in New Spending for Aboriginal People,' *CBC News*, Available from: http://www.cbc.ca/news/aboriginal/liberal-budget-billions-new-spending-aboriginal-peoples-1.3502942

Kluttz, D. and Fligstein, N. (2016) 'Varieties of Sociological Field Theory', in S. Abrutyn (ed) *Handbook of Contemporary Sociological Theory*, New York: Springer Publishing, pp 185–204.

Kropotkin, P. (2001) *L'entraide, un facteur d'évolution*, Montreal: Écosociété.

Lachapelle, M.D. (2019) 'Espaces d'autonomie et structures de contraintes: la mise en œuvre du projet Bâtiment 7 à Montréal', in P.-A. Tremblay, S. Tremblay and Sabrina Tremblay (eds) *Au-delà du cynisme, réinventer l'avenir des communautés*, Chicoutimi: Groupe de recherche et d'intervention régionales (GRIR), pp 69–88.

Laloux, F. (2014) *Reinventing Organizations: vers des communautés de travail inspirées*, Paris: Diateino.

Lam, A. (2024) 'How Inflation Took a Bite Out of Workers' Wages as They Rose Over the Past Decade', *CBC News*, 26 June, Available from: https://www.cbc.ca/news/business/workers-wages-inflation-2023-1.7213736

Lamant, L. (2016) *Squatter le pouvoir: les mairies rebelles d'Espagne*, Montreal: Lux.

Landemore, H. (2013) *Democratic Reason: Politics, Collective Intelligence, and the Rule of the Many*, Princeton: Princeton University Press.

Laplante, R. (1994) *Guyenne, village coopératif: la petite russie*, Cachan: École normale supérieure Cachan.

Latouche, S. (2011) *Décoloniser l'imaginaire: la pensée créative contre l'économie de l'absurde*, Lyon: Parangon.

Latouche, S. (2018) 'The Path to Degrowth for a Sustainable Society', in H. Lehmann (ed) *Factor X: Challenges, Implementation Strategies and Examples for a Sustainable Use of Natural Resources*, Berlin: German Environment Agency, pp 277–84.

Latouche, S. (2024) 'Communs, bien commun et décroissance', *Revue du MAUSS*, 1(61): 155–66.

Laville, J.-L. (2011) *Agir à gauche: l'économie sociale et solidaire*, Paris: Desclée de Brouwer.

Laville, J.-L. (2013) *L'économie solidaire: une perspective internationale*, Paris: Fayard.

Laville, J.-L. (2016) *L'économie sociale et solidaire: pratiques, théories, débats*, Paris: Points.

Lavoie, J. and Panet-Raymond, J. (2014) *La pratique de l'action communautaire* (3rd edn), Quebec: Presse de l'Université du Québec.

Le Goff, A. and Girard, C. (eds) (2010) *La démocratie délibérative: anthologie de textes fondamentaux*, Paris: Herman.

Le Parisien (2017) ' "Les gens qui ne sont rien": la petite phrase de Macron qui ne passe pas', 3 July, Available from: https://www.leparisien.fr/politique/macron-critique-pour-avoir-evoque-les-gens-qui-ne-sont-rien-02-07-2017-7105494.php

Lévesque, B. (2003) 'Vers un modèle québécois de seconde génération?', *Cahiers du CRISES*, ET0303, Available from: https://crises.uqam.ca/wp-content/uploads/2018/10/ET0303.pdf

Levine, M. (1994) *Guerrilla P.R.*, New York: Regan Books.

Lewis, E. and Slitine, R. (2016) *Le coup d'État citoyen: ces initiatives citoyennes qui réinventent la démocratie*, Paris: La Découverte.

Loreto, N. (2020) *Take Back the Fight: Organizing Feminism for the Digital Age*, Halifax: Fernwood Publishing.

Luxembourg, R. (1905) *The Mass Strike, the Political Party and the Trade Union*, Detroit: Marxist Educational Society of Detroit.

Macdonald, D. (2025) 'Company Men: CEO Pay in Canada in 2023', The Canadian Centre for Policy Alternatives, Available from: https://www.policyalternatives.ca/news-research/company-men/

Maillé, M.-È. and Batellier, P. (2017) *Acceptabilité sociale: sans oui, c'est non*, Montreal: Écosociété.

Malraux, A. (2002 [1966]) 'Speech Given on the Occasion of the Inauguration of the House of Culture at Amiens on 19 March 1966', in J. Ahearne (ed) *French Cultural Policy Debates*, London: Routledge, pp 55–61.

Manier, B. (2012) *Un million de révolutions tranquilles: comment les citoyens changent le monde*, Paris: Les liens qui libèrent.

McAdam, D. (1999) *Political Process and the Development of Black Insurgency, 1930–1970*, Chicago: University of Chicago Press.

McKeen, W. and Porter, A. (2003) 'Politics and Transformation: Welfare State Restructuring in Canada', in W. Clement and L.F. Vosko (eds) *Changing Canada: Political Economy as Transformation*, Montreal: McGill–Queen's University Press, pp 109–34.

Mintzberg, H. (2016) *Rééquilibrer la société: pour un renouvellement radical au-delà de la gauche, de la droite et du centre*, Montreal: Somme toute.

Mohanty, C.T. (1989) 'On Race and Voice: Challenges for Liberation Education in the 1990s', *Cultural Critique*, 14: 179–208.

Mondragon (nd) 'Areas of Interest', Available from: https://www.mondragon-corporation.com/centro-promocion/en/areas-of-interest/

Montreal Declaration on evaluation and social impact measurement (2019) Montreal: Territoires innovants en économie sociale et solidaire (TIESS), Available from: https://tiess.ca/medias/documents/TIESS_EVAL-MTL-Declaration_de_Montreal-EN.pdf

Moore, M.-L. and Riddell, D.J. (2015) 'Scaling Out, Scaling Up, Scaling Deep: Advancing Systemic Social Innovation and the Learning Processes to Support It', Montreal: McConnell Foundation.

Morales Hudon, A. and Sarrasin, R. (2019) 'Les mouvements sociaux comme forme de participation politique', in A.-C. Fourot, R. Léger and J.C. Nicolas Kenny (eds) *Le Canada dans le monde: acteurs, idées, gouvernance*, Montreal: University of Montreal Press, pp 99–120.

Muñoz, J.E. (2009) *Cruising Utopia: The Then and There of Queer Futurity*, New York: New York University Press.

National Inquiry into Missing and Murdered Indigenous Women and Girls (2019) 'Reclaiming Power and Place: The Final Report of the National Inquiry into Missing and Murdered Indigenous Women and Girls', Gatineau.

Neveu, E. (2011) *Sociologie des mouvements sociaux*, Paris: La Découverte.

Nussbaumer, J. and Moulaert, F. (2007) 'L'innovation sociale au cœur des débats publics et scientifiques', in J.-L. Klein and D. Davidson (eds) *L'innovation sociale. Émergence et effets sur la transformation de la société*, Quebec: University of Quebec Press, pp 71–88.

Oberschall, A. (1973) *Social Conflict and Social Movement*, Englewood Cliffs: Prentice Hall.

Office of the Correctional Investigator (2013) 'Annual Report of the Office of the Correctional Investigator, 2012–2013', PS100-2013E, Ottawa: Government of Canada.

Office of the Correctional Investigator (2022) 'Annual Report of the Office of the Correctional Investigator, 2021–2022', Ottawa: Government of Canada.

Olson, M. (2011) *Logique de l'action collective*, Brussels: Ed de l'Université de Bruxelles.

Ostrom, E. (1990) *Governing the Commons*, Cambridge: Cambridge University Press.

Palmater, P. (2019) 'Ellen Gabriel on Defending Kanehsatà:ke Mohawk Territory', August (Warrior Life podcast), Available from: https://soundcloud.com/pampalmater/ellen-gabriel-on-defending-kanehsatake-mohawk-territory

Pay Equity Office: Ontario (nd) 'The Gender Wage Gap: It's More Than You Think', Government of Ontario, Available from: https://payequity.gov.on.ca/the-gender-wage-gap-its-more-than-you-think/

Peck, J. and Tickell, A. (2002) 'Neoliberalizing Space', *Antipode*, 34(3): 380–404.

Pelletier, G. (1972) 'Democratization and Decentralization: A New Policy for Museums', *ICOM News*, 25(4): 219–22.

Peters, T.J. (1993) *L'entreprise libérée: Liberation Management*, Paris: Dunod.

Philip, M.N. (2008) *Zong!*, Middletown: Wesleyan University Press.

Piketty, T. (2013) *Le capital au XXIe siècle*, Paris: Seuil.

La Pointe libertaire (2013) *Bâtiment 7: victoire populaire à Pointe Saint-Charles*, Montreal: Écosociété.

Polyani, K. (2001 [1944]) *The Great Transformation*, Boston: Beacon Press.

Postone, M. (1993) *Time, Labor, and Social Domination: A Reinterpretation of Marx's Critical Theory*, Cambridge: Cambridge University Press.

Quatremère De Quincy, A.C. (1828) *De l'invention et de l'innovation dans les ouvrages des beaux-arts*, Paris: Firmin Didot.

Quijoux, M. (2011) 'Usines récupérées d'Argentine: des mobilisations ouvrières à dimension locale', *Cahiers des Amériques latines*, 66: 91–105.

Rabouin, L. (2009) *Démocratiser la ville: le budget participatif; de Porto Alegre à Montréal*, Montreal: Lux.

Réseau québécois en innovation sociale (2011) 'Déclaration québécoise pour l'innovation sociale'.

Reynolds, K. (2014) 'Disparity Despite Diversity: Social Injustice in New York City's Urban Agriculture System', *Antipode*, 47(1): 240–59.

Rivard, R. (1984) *Opening Up the Museum: Toward a New Museology; Ecomuseums and 'Open' Museums*, Quebec City: independently published, p 44, Reproduced with permission

Rivière, G.H. (1985) 'The Ecomuseum: An Evolutive Definition', *Museum International*, 37(4): 182–3.

Robert, C. and Toupin, L. (eds) (2018) *Le travail invisible: portrait d'une lutte féministe inachevée*, Montreal: Remue-ménage.

Robichaud, D. and Turmel, P. (2012) *La juste part: repenser les inégalités, la richesse et la fabrication des grille-pains*, Montreal: Atelier 10.

Robra, B., Heikkurinen, P. and Nesterova, I. (2020) 'Commons-Based Peer Production for Degrowth? The Case for Eco-Sufficiency in Economic Organisations', *Sustainable Futures*, 2: 100035.

Romeo, N. (2022) 'How Mondragon Became the World's Largest Co-Op', *The New Yorker*, 27 August.

Rosa, H. (2010) *Alienation and Acceleration: Towards a Critical Theory of Late-Modern Temporality*, Malmøgade: NSU Press.

Rosa, H. (2018) *Resonance: A Sociology of Our Relationship to the World*, Cambridge: Polity.

Rosa, H., Dörre, K. and Lessenich, S. (2017) 'Appropriation, Activation and Acceleration: The Escalatory Logics of Capitalist Modernity and the Crises of Dynamic Stabilization', *Theory, Culture & Society*, 34(1): 53–73.

Rosanvallon, P. (1976) *L'âge de l'autogestion: ou la politique en poste de commandement*, Paris: Seuil.

Roy, M., Bouchard, M., Fortin, É., Gruet, É., Huot, G. and Vézina, M. (2016) 'L'entrepreneuriat social et l'entreprise sociale: synthèse de connaissances', Montreal: TIESS.

Russell, A. and Vinsel, L. (2016) 'Hail to the Maintainers', *Aeon Magazine*, 7 April.

Saito, K. (2024) *Slow Down: The Degrowth Manifesto*, New York: Penguin Random House.

Say, J.-B. (1972 [1803]) *Traité d'économie politique, ou Simple exposition de la manière dont se forment, se distribuent ou se consomment les richesses*, Paris: Calmann-Lévy.

Schimanski, L.A. and Alperin, J.P. (2018) 'The Evaluation of Scholarship in Academic Promotion and Tenure Processes: Past, Present, and Future', *F1000research*, 7(1605): 1–21.

Schumpeter, J. (1942) *Capitalism, Socialism, and Democracy*, New York: Harper & Brothers.

Sedgwick, E.K. (2003) *Touching Feeling: Affect, Pedagogy, Performativity*, Durham, NC: Duke University Press.

Shang, L. and Chandra, Y. (2017) 'Anti-Oppression Practices in Social Enterprises', paper presented at the Sixth EMES International Research Conference on Social Enterprise, Université Catholique de Louvain.

Siltanen, J., Klodawsky, F. and Andrew, C. (2014) 'This Is How I Want to Live My Life: An Experiment in Prefigurative Feminist Organizing for a More Equitable and Inclusive City', *Antipode*, 17(1): 1–20.

Simpson, A. (2014) *Mohawk Interruptus: Political Life across the Borders of Settler States*, Durham, NC: Duke University Press.

Simpson, L.B. (2011) *Dancing on Our Turtle's Back: Stories of Nishnaabeg Re-creation, Resurgence, and a New Emergence*, Winnipeg: ARP Books.

Sintomer, Y. (2007) *Le pouvoir au peuple: jurys citoyens, tirage au sort et démocratie participative*, Paris: La Découverte.

Sintomer, Y., Herzberg, C. and Allegretti, G. (2014) 'Les budgets participatifs dans le monde: une étude transnationale', Bonn: Engagement Global.

Social Innovation and Social Finance Strategy Co-Creation Steering Group (2018) 'Inclusive Innovation: New Ideas and New Partnerships for Stronger Communities', Ottawa: Employment and Social Development Canada.

Solé, A. (2008) 'L'entreprisation du monde', in 'Repenser l'entreprise: saisir ce qui commence, vingt regards sur une idée neuve', *Possibles*, 40(2): 27–54.

Sorin, V. and Gruet, É. (2017) *Guide d'émission pour les entreprises d'économie sociale*, Montreal: TIESS.

Stambouli, J. (2021) 'L'avancée technologique sera l'ultime réponse aux enjeux de développement durable', in S. Baba (ed) *Trente idées reçues sur le développement durable*, Montreal: Editions JFD, pp 155–8.

Statistics Canada (2023) 'Prices and Inflation, Canada at a glance 2023', Government of Canada, Available from: https://www150.statcan.gc.ca/n1/pub/12-581-x/2023001/sec14-eng.htm

Stauber, J. and Rampton, S. (2002) *Toxic Sludge Is Good for You: Lies, Damn Lies and the Public Relations Industry*, Monroe: Common Courage Press.

Suyemoto, K.L., Donovan, R.A. and Kim, G.S. (2022) 'Understanding Power, Privilege, and Oppression', in *Unraveling Assumptions*, London: Routledge, pp 37–65.

Talpin, J. (2016) *Community organizing: de l'émeute à l'alliance des classes populaires aux États-Unis*, Paris: Raisons d'agir.

Tarasuk, V., Mitchell, A. and Dachner, N. (2014) 'L'insécurité alimentaire des ménages au Canada', Toronto: Research to identify policy options to reduce food insecurity (PROOF).

Theron, C. (2020) 'La consultation en innovation sociale', Masters Thesis, HEC Montréal.

TIESS (Territoires innovants en économie sociale et solidaire) (nd) 'Les impacts négatifs potentiels de la mesure d'impact', Available from: https://tiess.ca/outils/12-les-impacts-negatifs-potentiels-de-la-mesure-dimpact

Tilly, C. (1976) *From Mobilization to Revolution*, Reading: Addison-Wesley.

Tremblay, A. (2022) 'De l'Écomusée de l'au-delà fondé en 1991 à l'Écomusée du patrimoine funéraire et commémoratif fondé en 2022, l'aboutissement d'un long processus de réflexion', L'Écomusée du patrimoine funéraire et commémoratif, Available from: https://ecomuseedupatrimoine.org/ressources/trente-ans-devolution-2/

Truth and Reconciliation Commission of Canada (2015) 'Honouring the Truth, Reconciling for the Future: Summary of the Final Report of the Truth and Reconciliation Commission of Canada', Ottawa: Truth and Reconciliation Commission of Canada.

Tuck, E. and Yang, K.W. (2012) 'Decolonization Is Not a Metaphor', *Decolonization: Indigeneity, Education & Society*, 1(1): 1–40.

Tufekci, Z. (2020) 'Do Protests Even Work?', *The Atlantic*, 24 June.

Union of Ontario Indians (2013) 'An Overview of the Indian Residential School System', North Bay: Creative Impressions.

University of Guelph (2022) 'Building community: introduction to equity, diversity, and inclusion', Guelph, ON: Ecampus Ontario, Available from: https://ecampusontario.pressbooks.pub/buildingcommunityintrotoedi/front-matter/introduction/

Vercauteren, D. (2011) *Micro-politiques des groupes: pour une écologie des pratiques collectives*, Paris: Les Prairies ordinaires.

Walker, K. (2023) 'Manitoba's Reasons for Refusing to Search for Indigenous Women's Remains in Landfill Are a Smokescreen', The Conversation, 17 July.

Webber, M. and Butovsky, J. (2018) 'Faculty Associations Confront Accountability Governance in Ontario Universities', *Canadian Journal of Higher Education/Revue canadienne d'enseignement supérieur*, 48(3): 165–81.

Williams, R. (1959) 'Definitions of Culture', *New Statesman*, 25 July.

Withers, A.J. (2012) *Disability Politics and Theory*, Winnipeg: Fernwood Publishing.

Wright, E.O. (2010) *Envisioning Real Utopias*, New York: Verso.

Wright, E.O. (2019) *How to Be an Anticapitalist in the 21st Century*, New York: Verso.

Yunus, M. (2010) *Building Social Business: The New Kind of Capitalism that Serves Humanity's Most Pressing Needs*, New York: Public Affairs.

Zamora, D. and Görtz, N. (2014) 'Saul Alinsky: organiser le pouvoir populaire', Ballast, 12 December.

Index

References to figures appear in *italic* type; those in **bold** type refer to tables. References to endnotes show both the page number and the note number (168n28).

A

Aboriginal rights 53
abortion, right to 75, 79
Abraham, Yves-Marie 32, 104
activism 39, 56, 66, 72, 84, 155
activist legitimacy 37
adaptive stabilization 104–5
Adaptiveness of Tradition 53–5
administrative burden 154–5
Ahmed, Sarah 71
Albert, Michael 100, 101
Alfred, Taiaiake 52–6
Algonquin Anishinaabe Peoples 9
alienation 93, 96, 104
Alinsky, Saul 126–8
All Lives Matter framings 90
Al-Saji, Alia 50
Amis de VIO.ME (French organization) 124
animal rights movements 28
anti-essentialism 71
anti-oppression 63, 69–70, 121
antiracism 7, 68–70, 72, 73, 125
Antony, Wayne 41
archives, limits of 57, 60–1
Aristotle 130
Arnstein, Sherry 129
Arsenault, Gabriel 21–2
Ashoka Foundation 20, 110
Atelier 155–6
attribution, acts of 84
austerity 16, 19, 88–9, 143
Azoulay, Ariella Aïsha 57

B

Babyloan 112
Bacqué, Marie-Hélène 22–3, 128–9
#BalanceTonPorc 79
banking model of education (Freire) 149
Barcelona 133
Bâtiment 7 project, Montreal 23, 124–5, 168n28
Bauwens, Michel 103
belonging 35, 84, 140
Benford, Robert D. 85, 86
Bibak company 111–12
Biewener, Carole 22–3
Bilge, Sirma 65, 67
Bill C-45, Canada 80
Bishop, Matthew 20
black bloc 84
Black communities 40, 42, 46, 68, 78, 79, 84, 168n8
Black feminist movements 66–7
Black Indigenous and People of Colour (BIPOC) 72
Black Lives Matter 1–2, 90
blaming 83, 89–90, 165
Bloch, Ernst 59
block teaching 154
Blue Lives Matter framings 90
Boltanski, Luc 120
Book of Prayer 14
Bookchin, Murray 100, 132
borders and adversaries, framing of 85
Bouchard, Lucien 21, 89
Bourdieu, Pierre 25, 32, 34
bourgeoisie 58, 59, 108, 141

Index

Brodie, Janine 15, 42
brown, adrienne maree 72–3
Brown marginalized communities 72
Brownlee, Jamie 147, 148
business model and plan 109, 115, 116, 117
business-washing practice 117

C

Cabral, Amílcar 57–9
call-outs 72
Canadian Centre for Social Entrepreneurship 111
cancel culture 72
Cantillon, Richard 108
capital 14, 32–3, 34, 38, 48, 92, 101, 108, 111, 158
capitalism 17, 22, 27–8, 38, 46, 65, 96, 100, 103, 161, 162
 conscious capitalism 19
 evil capitalism 24
 and state communism dichotomy 122
 in transforming economy 92–4
capitalists
 economy 94–5
 enterprise and labor **97**, 97–8, 107
 entrepreneurs 93, 110
 system 22–3, 26, 48, 92, 93–4, 99, 101, 104, 162
Centre for Social Innovation, Toronto 116
Centre-Sud neighborhood 123, 139
changemakers 35, 36–7, 38
charity-based model of solidarity 41
Chavis, Benjamin 46
Chiapello, Eve 120
Chile 16
Cho, Sumi 66
choice frames 86
Christiania neighborhood of Copenhagen 123
citizen participation 22, 127, 129, 131
civic management, of public goods 133
civil rights movement, US 77–8
claiming 83, 85
classic private enterprise 118, 120
Clayoquot Sound 10
Cockshott, Paul 100
collaborative practices 1, 8, 18, 103, 119–20, 121, 130, 144, 148

collective action 4, 6, 22, 69, 71, 91, 107, 146, 159, 164, 166
collective mobilization 76
 community involvement 126–8
 frames 86
 reasons for 74–6
 repertoire of 77
 between social movements and innovations 80–2
 symbolic construction 83–5
collective identity 84
collective narratives 165
collective organizations 20, 120
Collins, Patricia Hill 65, 67
colonialism 22, 27–8, 58–9, 65, 67, 71, 142, 161
Combahee River Collective Statement 66
commodification 18, 19, 26–30
commodity production 50, 93–4
common good, idea of 102–3
common sense revolution 88
commons 23, 49, **97**, 101–3, 105
communism 8, 19, 105, 122, 138–44
Community Economic Development Investment Funds in Nova Scotia 80, 116
community gardens 102, 146
community involvement 4, 19, 80, 127–8, 158, 162
community land trust 49, 102
Confédération française démocratique du travail 122
consensus decision-making 34, 81, 120
contextual adaptation 52, 53, 55, 59–60
CoopCycle, France 122–3
cooperative model (Co-ops) 95, 112, 113–14, 132
corporate social responsibility 18, 111
corporatization 8–9, 19, 147
Cottrell, Allin 100
Coulthard, Glen 45–6
countermovement, of communities 27
COVID-19 pandemic 11–12, 105, 149
creative destruction 109
credibility 33, 37, 86
Crenshaw, Kimberlé 67

CRISES (Center for Research
  on Social Innovations
  at the University of
  Quebec-Montreal) 33–4
critical fabulation 60–1
critical race theory 6, 66
critical reflection 9, 11, 47, 154
critical thinking 4, 47, 63, 73, 150,
  151, 152, 154
crowdfunding 32–3, 116
cultural capital 32, 33, 65
cultural elites 135–6, 141
cultural genocide 81, 89,
  137, 174n7
culturally pluralist frames 86
culture 8, 134
  as a catalyst for better future 144–5
  community empowerment 138–44
  definition categories of 134–5
  of oppression 135–8
curators, and cultural narratives 141

D

Dardot, Pierre 16, 101
Davis, Angela 10, 49, 66
Days of Action in Ontario
  (1990) 10
De l'invention et de l'innovation
  dans les ouvrages des
  beaux-arts 13
de Varine, Hugues 142
Decidim Barcelona (digital
  platform) 133
decision-making 8, 61, 71–2, 81,
  105, 112, 115, 120,
  129–30, 137
decolonization 7, 28, 70–1, 73
defenders of freedom (hooks) 154
Dégnékoro commune, Mali 132
DeGraffenreid v. General Motors
  (1976) 67
degrowth communism 103–5
deindustrialization 139
democracy 23, 54–5, 119, 122, 124,
  150, 163, 164
  corporate 98
  deliberative 129–30
  democratic management 4, 126
  direct 81, 123, 131, 132
  and economic planning 100
  governance 112, 113–14, 118,
    125, 155
  organizations 3, 8, 93

participatory 128–30
return to democracy, frame 86, 90
social democratic social
  innovations 20–2, 26, 163
democratization 7, 98–101,
  103, 105
Dendra Systems company 112
Devine, Pat 100
diagnostic framing 85, 89
digital platforms 18, 79, 109, 112
discrimination 6, 31, 65, 66, 67, 84
dissident intellectuals 154
Dixon, Chris 47
documentary culture 134
domestic violence 79
domination 4–6, 16, 22, 27–8, 56,
  64, 84, 124–5, 136, 137, 141,
  152, 162
  colonial 50, 55
  direct and indirect 58
  resistance to 28
double movement thesis 26–7
Drayton, Bill 110
Dufort, Philippe 29, 30
Duggan, Mike 174n21(Ch 11)
dynamic stabilization, of
  society 104–5

E

ecomuseum 140, 142–4, *143*
economic capital 32–3
economic inequalities 16, 27, 93
economy transformation 92
  capitalism, in brief 92–4
  democratized economy 7, 98–101,
    103, 105
  different spheres of 94–6
  postcapitalist economy 97–8
  postgrowth societies 103–6
Élisabeth-Bruyère School of Social
  Innovation 3, 9, 18, 23, 29,
  114–15, 161–2
  rethinking pedagogy at 153–7
  social impact 159
  values and aspirations of 4–5
Elson, Diane 100
Éluard, Paul 49
emancipation 2–5, 22–3, 27–9,
  39, 42–3, 126, 146, 151,
  159, 163–5
empowerment 18, 22–3, 81, 110,
  127, 128, 162
Endenburg, Gerard 120

engaged research 147–50
Enterprising NonProfits 111
entrepreneurs 81, **97**, 107–9
  capitalists entrepreneurs 93, 110
  classic entrepreneurs 110, **111**, 114
  collective entrepreneurship 7, 112, 114, 116, 117, 132–3, 158
  emancipation and social entrepreneurship 2–5
  entrepreneurial legitimacy 37
  hero 109
  immigrant entrepreneurship 110
  industrial entrepreneurs 108
  as social change actor 110–12, **111**, 112, 158
  social impact, measuring 116–18
  starting new social organization 114–16
  wealthy entrepreneurs 93
environmental crisis 1, 50, 51
environmental justice 46–7, 81, 86
environmental pollutants 46
equality 1, 22, 41–4, 46, 74–5, 90, 120, 121
equity 42–3, 44, 69, 71, 73, 99, 138
erosion mechanism, in capitalism 27, 93
Euguélionne feminist bookstore, Montreal 122–3
exclusion 21, 22, 44, 46, 70, 84, 90, 142
exploitation 28, 93, 98, 124, 151
expropriation, and capitalism 93

F

fact-based object-suited Possible 59
factually-objectively Possible 59
farming co-ops 96, **97**, 123
Farrell, Nathan 19
feminism 7, 9, 66–8, 79, 121
field, as social innovation 32–5
Findhorn, Scotland 123
Fligstein, Neil 34, 35
Fontan, Jean-Marc 110–11, 148
Ford, Henry 107, 108
formally Possible 59
framing 85–8
France 20, 45, 90, 104, 122, 123, 136, 138
Franco-Ontarian community 88–9, 144
Fraser, Nancy 5, 25, 27–8, 29, 30, 44–5, 93–4

Fraser Valley Centre for Social Enterprise 111
free market society 27
free rider role 75
Freire, Paulo 8, 126, 149, 150–1, 153
Fuckup Night movement 165
funding 7, 17, 20, 21, 37–8, 115–16, 118, 158
  crowdfunding 32–3, 116
  public funding 10
  in research 147–8
funerary heritage of Montreal 139–40

G

Gabriel, Ellen 55
Gandhi, Mohandas Karamchand 10
Gayanerekowa [Kaianere'kó:wa] 55
gender equity 44
Gender-Based Analysis Plus 68–9
Gibson-Graham, J.K. 48, 97
global financial crisis of 2007–08 17
global warming 104
Godin, Benoît 14
Goffman, Erving 85
Gordillo, Juan Manuel Sánchez 123
Gorz, André 96
Gramsci, Antonio 47–8
Grand Costumier 116
grassroots initiatives 15, 20, 66, 70, 119, 126, 128–31, 132
Great Depression 10
Great Law of Peace 54
Green, Michael 20
Greenpeace 87
grieving optimism 47–8
gross domestic product (GDP) 98–9, 104
Guerilla PR 87
Gurr, Ted 76
Guyenne, Quebec 132

H

habitus 32, 33
Hahnel, Robin 100, 101
Hall, Louis Karoniaktajeh 54, 55
Hardt, Michael 56
Harnecker, Marta 100
Harper, Stephen 42
Harris, Mike 88
Hartman, Saidiya 60–1
hashtag activism 1, 45, 78, 79

hegemonic frames 86
heteropatriarchy 65, 67, 161
heterosexism 44, 48, 50, 66, 67
Hickel, Jason 104
hierarchical organization 119, 120, 121, 124
hippy communes 123
Homo economicus 15–16
hooks, bell 8, 154
  classroom practice and critical thinking 152–3
  transgressive pedagogy 147–9
hooligans, protestors characterized as 84, 85
horizontal organizations 58, 119, 120
houses of culture (Malraux) 136
housing crises 50
human rights 55, 67–8, 80, 81, 126

I

ideal culture 134–5
identity(ies) 31, 44–5, 54, 65, 67, 84–5, 90, 140, 142, 143, 144
Idle No More movement 1–2, 80, 89
imaginations 60–2, 103, 109, 121, 164
imperialism 57–8
income units 148
Indigenous people 9, 40–2, 53, 67, 72
  colonial violence against 42, 70
  cultural genocide 89, 137
  decolonization movements 28
  harassment and sexual violence 44–5
  Indigenous commons 102
  mobilization 7, 80–1, 125
  redistribution and recognition 44–6
  resurgence and regeneration process 52–6
  rights, violations and abuses of 67–8
individualism 17
Industrial Revolution 77
inflation, impact of 40
information and communication technologies revolution 14
injustice frames 86
institutional legitimacy 37
institutional recognition 21, 148

institutionalization 21, 36–7, 93
intentional communities 23, 123, 124
interdependence 34, 35, 121
intermediary organizations 37–8
internal governance units 35, 38
International Cooperative Alliance 113
International Council of Museums (ICOM) 136, 138
interpretive frameworks 34, 37–8
intersectionality 65–70, 72–3
interstitial transformations 9, 162
Iroquois Confederacy 54
Italy 20, 123

J

Jackson, Mississippi 132
Jobs, Steve 108–9
Just Recovery for All 11–12, *12*

K

Kaepernick, Colin 30, 168n8
Kahnawà:ke community 53–4, 55, 56
Kahnawa'keró:non 53–4
Kanehsatà:ke community 55
Kenney, Annie 79
King, Martin Luther 10, 78
Kinsman, Gary 10
Kropotkin, Peter 122
Kurdish democratic confederalism, in Syria 132

L

labor 48, 92, 93, **96**, **97**, 120, 121
labor force, division of 95–6, 109
labor market and school system, link between 124
labor movements 7, 122
labor of care, gendered 93
ladder of citizen participation (Arnstein) 129
land development initiatives, innovative 132
Landless Workers' Movement cooperatives, Brazil 160–1
Larzac struggle 123
Latin America 20, 130
Latouche, Serge 104
Laval, Christian 16, 101
Laville, Jean-Louis 20
l'Écomusée du fier monde 139

l'Écomusée du patrimoine funéraire et commémoratif (EPFC) 140, 143–4
liberation 15, 43, 46, 49, 56, 148, 152, 154
　African liberation struggles 57–8, 60
　Black liberation struggles 28, 132
　equality and equity, story-based strategy 42–3
　of nation 57–60
　of women 79
liberatory social innovation 22–4, 31, 41, 48, 74, 81, 125, 166
libertarian municipalism 132
linguistic rights 89
LIP (watch-making company), France 122
little Russia 132
logic of rupture 162
Lorde, Audre 66
Luxemburg, Rosa 11

M

macrosocial-level change 27, 30, 38, 83, 159, 161
Malraux, André 136
marginalization 65, 66, 67
marginalized groups 22, 44, 70, 72, 131, 158, 162
　exclusion of 46
　grassroots participation 128–9
　self-organization of 126
Marinaleda, Andalusia 123
market economy 37, 92, 94–5, 97, 99, 118
market resources, school of 111
market socialism 100
marketization 5
marriage equality 44
Marx, Karl 6, 105
Marxism–Leninism 105
master frames 86, 89
mausoleums 139–40
McAdam, Doug 34, 35
McConnell Foundation 20, 111
Mead, Margaret 126
mesosocial organizations 37–8
#MeToo movement 1–2, 45, 78, 79
Michi Saagiig Nishnaabeg 71
microcredit 20, 112
microsocial level organization 21, 35, 36, 38
migrant rights 75

Mills, Wright C. 63
mission drift *see* strategic drift of organizations
mobilization 1–2, 75–6, 85–6, 160
　civil rights movement in US 77–8
　incidents 10, 77–8, 88–9
　Indigenous mobilizations and call-out 80–1
　mass mobilizations 74–5, 146
　"plaza" movement 81
　sit-ins 78
　tactics, circulation of 78–9
　women's movement 78–9
Mohanty, Chandra Talpade 8, 150, 151, 153
Mohawks of Kahnawake 54
Mondragon Corporation, Spain 113–14
Montfort Hospital, mobilization to save 88–9
Montgomery bus boycott campaign 77–8
Montgomery Improvement Association 78
Montreal Declaration on evaluation and social impact measurement 118
Moore, Michele-Lee 160
motivational framing 85
Moulaert, Frank 17
Muhammad Yunus Social Business 20, 111
municipal budget 130–1
municipal policy transition 131–3
municipalism 132–3, 163
Muñoz, José Esteban 57
Muttart and McConnell Foundations 111
mutual aid groups 1, 3, 8, 38, 48, 80, 94, 96, 105, 124
　and evolution 122
　horizontal organizations 119
　and movements 81
　neighborhood groups 11, 123, 139
　and neoliberalism 17
　and social economy 20
　women-only online groups 79
myth of verticality 119–21

N

naming a problem 83, 89, 165
National Confederation of Labor 122

national cultural heritage 137
National Gallery 136–7
National Inquiry into Missing and Murdered Indigenous Women and Girls 42, 67
national museums, and legislation 134, 136–7
neocolonialism 58–9, 60
neoliberalism 5, 22, 23, 101, 123
 response to 15–18
 social 18–20
neoliberalization of university 8–9, 19, 147
 engaged research 147–50
 reflections on university practice 150–3
Neopenda, Uganda 112
Neveu, Erik 76, 84
Nishnaabeg culture 71
#NiUnaMenos 79
no-growth economy 104
nongovernmental organizations (NGOs) 60, 80, 95
nonparticipation, of citizens 129
nonprofit organizations 99, 102, 111
North America 3, 10, 82, 130, 171n10(Ch 6)
Nussbaumer, Jacques 17

O

Oberschall, Anthony 77
objectively-real Possible 59
Olson, Mancur 75
On invention and innovation in the fine arts (Quatremère de Quincy) 13
One House Many Nations campaign 81
Oneka 112
Onkwehonwe resurgence 53, 55–6
Ontario Trillium Drug Program 10
oppositional frames 96
oppression 3, 6, 8, 9, 29, 46, 48, 72, 125, 127, 151, 153, 159, 164–5, 166
 culture of 135–8
 and emancipation 27–8
 and intersectionality 65–8
 and privileges 64–5
 structural 63–5, 71
organizational paradoxes 29–30
Ostrom, Elinor 101

P

Palmater, Pam 70
Pankhurst, Christabel 79
Paris Commune (1871) 122, 132
Paris suburb riots (2005) 77
Parks, Rosa 10, 78
Parti socialiste unifi (Unified Socialist Party) 122
participatory budget 128, 155, 163
participatory research 148–9
partnership research 148
past, looking at the 50–2
 Adaptiveness of Tradition 53–4, 55
 imagination 60–2
 restaging past hopes and anticipation 56–60
 resurgence and regeneration process 52–6
 and ways of transforming present 52
patriarchy 28, 66
peasant revolts, in Europe 77
Peck, Jamie 19
pedagogy 8–9, 146–7, 164
 committees of professors 154
 in daily life 150–3
 at Élisabeth-Bruyère School of Social Innovation 153–7
 emancipatory pedagogy 151
 liberatory pedagogy 4–5
 as praxis for social transformation 148–51
 radical pedagogy 150, 152
 theoretical texts 154
 and training, by self-management 123–5
 transgressive pedagogy 147
Pelletier, Gérard 136–7
pertinence, significance of 86
philanthrocapitalism 20, 117
Philip, NourbeSe M. 60
Piketty, Thomas 167n8
Pinochet, Augusto 16
plural economy 94–6, 98, 99
Pointe-Saint-Charles, neighborhood in Montreal 23
Polanyi, Karl 5, 15, 25–7, 28, 29, 30
popular education 126–7, 128, 161
populism 90
Porto Alegre, participatory budget of 130–1
positive thinking 47

Index

possibility, layers of the category 59–60
postcapitalism 23, 97–8, 103
postgrowth societies 103–6
power 64, 65, 72–3, 127–8
praxis, and intersectionality 68–70
prefiguration 47–8, 49, 154
private economy 95
private enterprises 20–1, 98, 99, 111
private ownership 92
privilege 33, 64–5, 69–70, 72, 84, 135, 152, 155
professions of social innovation 36
prognostic framing 85
project initiator 107
project leaders 36
property rights 102
protests 1–3, 23, 57, 71, 74–9, 81–4, 107–8, 159
Proudhon, Pierre-Joseph 122
public economy 94–5
public museum model 140, 141–2, *142*
public relations 87–8
publications 89, 100, 101, 144, 148, 149
public–private partnerships 16

Q

Quatremère de Quincy, Antoine-Chrysostome 13

R

racism 22, 27–8, 46, 50, 51, 64, 66–7, 79, 161
  environmental 46
  in public transport 77–8
  and sexism, on Black women 67
  structural 69
  systemic 69
radical imagination 49, 50, 56–7
reactivating imaginaries 165
Reagan, Ronald 16
real utopias strategy (Wright) 49, 97–8, 106
Red Vienna (1918–34) 132
redistribution and recognition 44–6
reflexivity 6, 69, 73, 153, 164–5
reform 9, 55–6, 97–8, 141, 159, 162, 163, 164
regeneration 19, 52, 53–5
regional innovations 8
relative frustration 76

Religious Society of Friends 120
remunicipalization 133
Reseau quebecois en innovation sociale 161
residential school system, cultural genocide by 137
resilience 71, 104, 132, 162–4, 165
resistance strategy 163
resonance 35, 37, 38, 39, 86, 90, 164, 165–6
resurgence 1, 23, 26, 45–6, 52–6, 57, 60, 71
Reynolds, Kristin 41
Riddell, Darcy J. 160
Rivard, René 141, 142
Rivière, Georges Henri 142
Rosa, Hartmut 35, 105, 166
Russian Revolution (1905–17) 122

S

Saint-Basile-le-Grand, Quebec 131
Saint-Camille, Quebec 132
Saito, Kohei 105
Samuelson, Les 41
Say, Jean-Baptiste 108
scaling innovations, forms of 159–60, 162, 165
Schumpeter, Joseph 108–9
Sea Shepherd 87
Sedgwick, Eve 51
self-determination 54
self-governance 120
self-help 19
self-identification 84
self-management 4, 8, 98, 102, 103, 119–21, 133, 158
  collective 153
  and economic democracy 100
  history of 121–3
  training and pedagogy, learning by 123–5
self-organization 3, 17, 20, 22, 81, 107, 126
self-production 96
self-regulating market 26
sexism 22, 28, 51, 66, 67
sexual terrorism frames 86
Shotwell, Alexis 47
Silicon Valley 109, 165
Simpson, Audra 45
Simpson, Leanne Betasamosake 71
slavery 61
"small is beautiful" strategy 165

Snow, David A. 85, 86
social and solidarity economy (SSE) 20, 95, 112, 113–14, 162
social businesses 18, 20, 111
social capital 32
social cohesion 21, 27, 110, 162
social economy 15, 18, 20–2, 36, 39, 80, 95–6, 98, 102, 119
  collective enterprises 20–1, 23, 95, **97**, 114, 116, 118, 158, 160–1, 162
  democratic transformation of 132
  enterprises 80, 96, 110–12, 160
  institutionalization of 21–2
  limitations, consideration of 98–9, 111, 112
  market activities 95–6, 160
  social-democratic vision 21
social effects, notion of 27, 28, 29, 30–1, 38, 151
social enterprises 4, 7, 18–21, 31, 94, 111, 112, 117, 121
social entrepreneurship 2–5, 3, 7, 18, 20, 32, 36, 39, 110–12, 158
social finance 36, 117
social franchise 160
social impact 23, 29, 39, 158–9, 160
  and capitalism 19
  of local initiatives 26
  measurement of 9, 20, 26, 116–18
  see also social effects, notion of
social inequalities 1, 3, 6, 15, 41, 61, 92, 104, 109
social injustice 22, 46, 69–70, 76, 166
social justice 20, 38, 41, 42–6, 107, 131, 148, 156, 159, 163
  antiracism and anti oppression framework 69
  and the past 60
  prefiguration of 47–9
  transformative justice 71–3
social media 72, 78, 79, 87, 130
social movements 1–7, 26, 69, 71, 74–6, 128, 160
  and discursive strategies 88–91
  framing 85–8
  identity dimension 84
  and innovations 80–2
  and mobilization 75–80
  symbolic construction of 83–5
social organization, process for starting a 114–16

social organizing of forgetting (Kinsman) 10
social practices 3, 17, 18, 22, 48
social protection 5, 21, 26–9
social reproduction 93, 94, 95, 96, 99
social safety net 16, 19
social struggles 26, 28, 39, 75, 82
social systems 161–2
  dismantling 163
  escaping from 162
  four Rs to change 163
  resistance strategy 163
  strategies 162–4, **164**
  taming the system 163
sociocracy 120, 125
Sociocracy Group 125
sociopolitical purpose of organizations 29
solidarity economy 23, 95–6, 112
  see also social and solidarity economy (SSE)
sovereignty movement 53
Spanish Revolution (1936) 122
spin-offs strategy 160
Sprott Centre for Social Enterprises 111
start-ups 109, 158, 165
state economy 95
steady-state economy 104
strategic action fields 34–5
strategic approach, to social innovation 25–6
  Fligstein and McAdam's approach 34–5
  Fraser and the emancipation movement 27–8
  organizational paradoxes 29–30
  Polanyi and the double movement 26–7
  social effects 29
  social innovation field 32–4, 36–9
strategic drift of organizations 30–2
strategies in politics 90–1, 132
structural inequality 64, 92, 160
student strike in Quebec (2012) 85
Students for a Democratic Society, United States 122
suffragettes 78–9
Summit on the Economic and Social Future of Quebec (1996) 21
sustainable development 103, 140

symbiotic transformation 9, 162
symbolic capital 32, 33, 38
symbolic construction of the social 83–5, 91
symbolic cooperation 129
symbolic gestures 87
syncretism 54, 56

T

tactical innovations 78–82, 83
technology and innovation, symbiotic relationship between 14–15, 93, 110
tendency toward crisis 93–4
Thatcher, Margaret 16, 167n7
theory of change 53
Thèsez-vous 116
Tickell, Adam 19
Tilly, Charles 77
tiny homes 81, 171n10(Ch 6)
Tito regime 122
tools of, in public relations 87–8
Touski Restaurant 123
toxic waste disposal 46
traditional hierarchical model 120–1
trans people
  gender-affirming care for 75
  rights of 82
transformative justice 63, 71–3
transphobia 67
Tremblay, Alain 143–4
Tricofi textile factory, Quebec 122
triple movement 28, 29, 31, 38
Trudeau, Pierre Elliott 136–7
Truth and Reconciliation Commission of Canada 89, 174n7
Tuck, Eve 70
Tufekci, Zeynep 82
Turtle Island, Canada 9
Twin Oaks, Virginia 123
2SLGBTQIA+ 9, 28, 40, 67, 167n1(Ch 1)

U

United Kingdom 16, 104
United States 16, 46, 77–8, 132, 168n8

V

Vanier Museopark, Ottawa 144
VIO.ME, Greece 124
vote, right to 78–9

W

wage labor 48, 92, 93, **96**, 121
White liberal feminism 66
White supremacy 67, 69
Williams, Raymond 134–5
Winnipeg General Strike (1919) 10
women-only online mutual aid groups 79
Workers' History Museum, Ottawa 138–9
workers' movement 23, 77, 161
world in crisis, in general 1–2, 11
World March of Women (2000) 70
Wright, Erik Olin 9, 49, 97–8, 100, 162–4

X

xenophobia 51

Y

Yang, K. Wayne 70
yellow vest movement, France 45
Yes Men 87
Young Foundation 20
Yugoslavian model of decentralized socialism 122
Yunus, Muhammad 20, 111, 167n17

Z

ZAD (zone à défendre), France 123
zero deficit policy 21

www.ingramcontent.com/pod-product-compliance
Lightning Source LLC
Chambersburg PA
CBHW051544020426
42333CB00016B/2088